"Kevin Cross's remarkab... ...y of redemption is told here with humor, tragedy, and love. You will root for him at his lowest point and cheer as he searches for the right path to redemption. Kevin has not only written a true crime story, but he inspires you to accomplish whatever you wish to accomplish. *Embezzlement* is an inspirational and uplifting book."
**Sheriff Nick Navarro**, Retired

"It has been my privilege to become acquainted with Kevin Cross. The book that he has written, *Embezzlement*, outlines in a very compelling way a unique story of Kevin's life from riches to rags to riches. Kevin is a great communicator, and I can recommend this book enthusiastically."
**Ron Blue**, President, Kingdom Advisors

"Kevin Cross is a living example of how far we can fall in this life, but, more importantly, he is an example of how far we can rise. The way God took him from living on the edge of death to living on the edge of the miraculous is truly inspirational. *Embezzlement* is a stunning achievement and I highly recommend it to anyone looking for inspiration or just a great read."
**Dr. Crawford W. Loritts, Jr.**
Author, Speaker, Radio Host
Senior Pastor of Fellowship Bible Church, Roswell, GA

"Kevin Cross has written a rare thing—a taut, true crime thriller that will change the way you think about your money and inspire you to do more with your life. The account of his life is nothing short of extraordinary. God miraculously shook him from his greed-filled daze and shaped him into the man he is today. Do yourself a favor and read this book."
**Howard Dayton**, Author
Founder of Crown Financial Ministries

# embezzlement
## A TRUE CRIME STORY

BY

# Kevin Cross

WITH STEVEN WHITE

BRIDGE
LOGOS
FOUNDATION

Alachua, Florida 32615

**Bridge-Logos**
Alachua, FL 32615 USA

**Embezzlement**
by Kevin Cross and Steven White

Edited by Kent Crockett

Printed in the United States of America.

Library of Congress Catalog Card Number: 2010921278
International Standard Book Number 978-0-88270-182-0

Unless otherwise indicated, Scripture quotations in this book are taken from the *Holy Bible, New International Version®*. NIV®. Copyright © 1973, 1978, 1984 by International Bible Society. Used by permission of Zondervan. All rights reserved.

Scripture quotations marked NASB are taken from the *New American Standard Bible*. Copyright © 1960, 1962, 1963, 1968, 1971, 1972, 1973, 1975, 1977, 1995 by The Lockman Foundation. Used by permission.

Scripture quotations marked MSG are taken from *The Message*. Copyright ©1993, 1994, 1995, 1996, 2000, 2001, 2002. Used by permission of NavPress Publishing Group.

G218.316.N.m1001.35240

## DEDICATION

To those who are being crushed under the weight of the
American Dream.

# ACKNOWLEDGMENTS

God has surrounded me with incredible people, both saints and scoundrels, who have shaped my life in awesome ways, some with brute force and others with gentleness. I'm overwhelmingly thankful for my mother and father, my loving wife Stephanie, who is my quiet strength, and my wonderful children, Ethan and Rachel, who teach me more than I teach them.

I am grateful as well for my best friend, partner in ministry, and fellow sojourner, Steven White, without whom none of this would be possible.

I'm eternally indebted to my betrayer, the FBI, the Sheriff's Department, my kidnappers, and my cellmates, all of whom worked, unwittingly, to finally awaken me from my state of confusion.

Special thanks go out as well to my publisher Lloyd Hildebrand, acquisitions editor Peggy Hildebrand, art director Elizabeth Nason, sales & marketing director Steve Becker, editor Kent Crockett, publicist Shawn Meyers, and the entire team at Bridge-Logos Publishers for their tireless work on this project.

# CONTENTS

# PREFACE

The story you are about to read is true. The names of some individuals have been changed to protect their identities.

My life story involves all the trappings of greed, betrayal, and the quest for happiness. We're all desperately grasping for something better as we travel through life. We buy the next big thing, or look to religion, celebrity, or sex to find some kind of satisfaction. Just when we think we've gotten hold of something and tighten our grip, it invariably slips through our fingers.

After all my mistakes, I discovered that crime really does pay—just not in the wages we would like.

Kevin Cross

# CHAPTER 1

# hatching the plan

At 10 P.M., the band Husker Dü, or some lesser imitation, was set to perform at the PBA Hall in Fort Lauderdale. It was Friday, which meant my buddy, Paul Johnson, would give me a ring to tell me where we'd hang out. Paul's dashing good looks invariably lifted me into the next social echelon of girls, clubs, and night life of Miami in the 1980s.

I was like a pauper who had climbed up the wall and gazed into a pastel-streaked Promised Land of chic clothes, drugs, drinks, fast cars, and even faster women. I peered in awesome wonder at the life-giving satisfaction that could be mine, and Paul was my ticket.

His looks were in stark contrast to mine. Where I was tall, lanky, and awkwardly formed, his physique was sculpted. He sported a shock of jet black hair, and had eyes the kind of transcendent blue that melted girls' hearts. He was my best friend and we were inseparable, but I always harbored a little jealousy against him for this.

"Hey Kev, what's doing tonight? We goin' out or what?" Paul asked from the other end of the line.

"Donny told me that some boss punk band is playing the PBA across from my office," I told Paul.

"You think there'll be chicks there?" Paul asked with the anticipation of a guy who actually had a chance.

"Of course. You know how it is. Girls with green hair, no hair, nose rings, safety pins, and ripped clothes. Our kind of girls. I'm totally amped."

My sarcasm knew no equal.

"Rad. I'll book it over there by ten o'clock," Paul said.

We had to hang up quickly as we were both at work. I worked as an accountant in the Civil Division of the Sheriff of Broward County, and Paul was a teller at Coral Gables Federal Savings and Loan in the very chic 163rd Street Mall. Our insatiable and unswerving pursuit of money, and all the trappings that came with it, was what united us. When it came to chasing pleasure, all bets were off. We were rabid social Darwinists and determined to be the fittest. We wholeheartedly bought into Gordon Gekko's famous quote from the film *Wall Street* that "greed is good." We pursued our careers with the voracity and hunger of two starved lions. The world owed us.

Paul came from a broken family. His mom's second husband was emotionally and physically abusive, which drove Paul and his younger sister into a closer relationship than most siblings. He watched the innocence that is the birthright of every child being taken from her and vowed to protect her at any cost. But there was only so much he could do. He would rise before the sun, even on weekends, and return late to insure a lesser sentence from his tyrant stepfather.

My circumstances were better than Paul's. My father Ray had a short fuse, which was probably a perfectly natural trait for a man with his background. He spent most of his young life in Philadelphia with his older sister, being shuffled between abusive foster homes. At the age of fifteen, he escaped from the St. Joseph's Industrious Home for Young Boys, and went straight to an Army recruiter's office with a note from his sister swearing he was seventeen years old.

The recruiter gave him fifty cents and told him he needed to gain five pounds before he could join. My dad went to a Philly hot dog stand, bought a half dozen or so, devoured them, and returned to the recruiter twenty minutes later with five pounds of hot dogs in his stomach. Before long, he was on the ground, fighting in Korea, and witnessing things no fifteen-year-old should ever see.

He returned from the war and worked his way up to a sales executive position in Philadelphia, a position he held for nearly twenty years. When he and my mother moved to South Florida in the 1960s, there was no work to be found. After a few years of searching and working an assortment of jobs, he was finally hired in the Civil Division of the Sheriff's Office of Broward County, where he watched four sheriffs come and go. He pulled some strings to get me a job in the same department.

He was a man cut from the fabric of an older generation that valued hard work and consistency over sensitivity, so spending countless hours coddling his children was not his first priority. That is not to say he was absent from my life. He just had the mindset of a man born in Philadelphia during the Great Depression. He possessed a kind of quiet strength only seen in those who live through genuinely hard times.

His sternness was tempered, though, by a quick wit, which I constantly but unsuccessfully tried to keep up with. His humor was in the dry and self-effacing vein, so he ingratiated himself to others with ease.

Marge, my mother, worked her way up from an entry level position at Hollywood Memorial Hospital to head of the lab there. She was long suffering and doted on all her children obsessively, making sure we were always sufficiently fed and clothed. Her work at the hospital meant she was on her feet all day dealing with who knows what, but somehow she always had enough energy for her four kids: Karen, Cindy, Kirk, and myself. She wanted to do everything for us and was always filled with a million questions about what we were doing and how we were doing it. Her day always began early; making breakfast, getting her kids to school an hour before her shift began, and picking them up an hour or two after it ended.

She and my father had been married for twenty-five years and the marriage was not always perfect. They tried their best to hide it, but I was a witness to many fierce arguments between them. It was a small house, and from my room I could hear everything that went on. I always acted as the pacifier; I would try to appease them and keep the mood light whenever I could. I was uncomfortable with any type of confrontation, and I developed a keen awareness of any brewing discord.

Money was always tight, but my mother knew a million tricks to keep our clothes tailored and stretch the food to feed a family of six. Some of her techniques met with our protests, and almost always clashed with our desires to look cool and keep up with the fashions popular at the time.

I was the youngest of four kids, which meant I was always the last in line for the hand-me-downs. I begrudgingly went to school with an unusual hodgepodge look of less-than-stylish clothes and shoes. Instead of the Reeboks most kids sported, I went with the off-brand sweater vest and sneakers my brother Kirk had worn for two years before me. I would sometimes rip them, or put clothespins in them in an attempt to appear "punk," but my mother would unfailingly sew them back up and return them to my drawer, perfectly folded.

This was forever my burden and my battle. I always unwillingly operated on the outside of what was considered cool, always one or two steps behind chic. I longed to be a part of it all. Everyone else I saw seemed unaffected by this affliction. They always seemed to be having so much fun. Their lives appeared so worthy of my admiration.

I finished work at the Sheriff's Office around nine, and decided to stroll across the street to the PBA Hall to see if our mutual friend Donny Beck had arrived. Donny "Rocket" was our longtime buddy and held the position in our circle as chief cultural advisor. He always knew where to find the bands, the brands, and the booze.

Donny chased after every girl that came within his radius, but he was desperately in love with two girls: Shawna, a brunette whom the rest of the guys would call Ka-reem due to her excessive height, and Jules, a delicate and shy blonde with emerald green eyes. He loved to clue us in to what we should be doing and saying to keep up with the masses. In these circles, it could be social suicide to make a faux-pas, like saying a band or club or style was radical, when it was decidedly not.

Donny was part of our group, but also operated outside of it. He was a lone wolf and would mysteriously disappear, sometimes for weeks. Then he'd reappear with the grandiose tales of his conquests and excursions into Miami's clandestine nightlife.

I ditched the glasses, tossed the tie, and un-tucked the button-down oxford, which was my monkey suit. I had to tone it down a little to avoid being tagged with the worst of all possible labels at the time, the dreaded *poser*—the guy who wears skate clothes, carries a skateboard, but doesn't know how to skate. In my case, it was the one pierced ear and work clothes that would give me away if I wasn't careful in this world.

The punk rock world in Miami in 1988 was simply a relic from the movement that had ignited Great Britain and New York in the late 1970s. At this point, even "punk" was being eschewed in favor of the rawer movement called "hardcore." Hardcore bands rejected any commercial success, and shunned punk bands for selling out. Bands like The Roidz, The Raging Pus Bags, People's Court, and the Doldrums dominated the local scene. Most of the patrons of these fine establishments were ones who had survived all the bandwagon folks, and counted themselves among the chosen.

And this counter-culture, like every one before it, had a uniform: the "safety-pin aesthetic," if you will. Metal-studded and spiked accessories poked through every available flap of skin.

Mohawks of every size and color proudly displayed themselves like giant peacock feathers. Vagabond-chic, hand-me-down jackets and jeans hung loosely on everyone's snarling, slouching bodies. It was an eerie spectacle to one unaccustomed to this brand of flamboyance.

I yearned to be part of this counter-culture, but I suffered from an intense feeling of inadequacy. I felt like the old joke: "I would hate to belong to any club that would accept me as a member." It was this innate desire burning inside of me to "fit in" that gave birth to "Ramone Simone." Ramone was an alter ego that I created and became, whenever being Kevin Cross didn't get me enough respect. He was a human chameleon, who took on the uniform and personality of whatever scene was the object of my envy.

The first incarnation of Ramone was a punk; complete with ripped T-shirt and jeans, leather jacket, spiked hair, and confident swagger. I would use my brother's old driver's license to get into clubs and introduce myself as Ramone Simone, a graduate student at Nova University. I once met a girl at a club called City Limits in Fort Lauderdale, and I carried on a six-month relationship with her as Ramone Simone, punk-about-town.

This was Freud's idea of the id, the ego, and the super-ego, in its purest form. The id is that part of our psyche that selfishly seeks pleasure and personal goals regardless of others. It is amoral and its only concern is fulfilling our deepest desires in spite of societal restraints. The super ego is the antithesis of the id and acts as a conscience, telling us what is acceptable behavior, and punishing us with feelings of guilt when we behave improperly. The ego is what helps us decide between the id and the super-ego, and is responsible for fulfilling the desires of the id in an acceptable and realistic way.

Ramone Simone was the personification of my id. He was the part of me who could be all the things Kevin Cross was incapable of, like having the confidence to talk to girls, or telling people what I really thought about them. This night, however, I was just Kevin.

Entering the club, I immediately spotted Donny's wiry frame and ghost-white skin wafting through the crowd of punk rockers. I began to make my way across the room to him, sidestepping the plebeians eyeing me with particular disdain, and being careful to avoid the mosh pit of people slam-dancing. For the uninitiated, slam-dancing consists of repeatedly hurling your body into a fellow patron with as much force as you can muster until sufficiently mind-numbed.

Our usual hangout, Perone's, had closed a few weeks earlier, and the PBA Hall was the first candidate for a replacement spot. These kinds of clubs wore their filthiness like a badge of honor. The filthier your bar was, the more legitimate. I always suspected they employed a whole crew of anti-janitors, guys who came in the mornings to spread dirt, write on the wall, and paint like a blind person. The PBA had all this charm, but you couldn't get away with bringing your own beer like we could at Perone's and Fire and Ice, which was a huge negative for us poor kids.

We would buy a bunch of the cheapest beer imaginable, usually Schafers, and smuggle it in using our baggy jeans and leather jackets. We found a way around that quickly, inventing what we called "The Breakfast of Champions," a well-balanced meal consisting of Cheerios and cheap vodka. We would furiously eat as many spoonfuls as we could before entering the club. We theorized that the vodka-soaked Cheerios would sit in our stomachs and absorb more slowly, drawing out the intoxication, and eliminating the need to buy over-priced beers or liquor.

"Donny!" I screamed over the noise. "Donnyyyy!"

Finally, I got his attention and he pulled me into a dingy corner of the club where we would wait for Paul. Donny grabbed my arm and pulled me down so he could talk into my ear.

"S'up, Kev? You see that girl by the bar? She was totally checking me out, dude. She's a total betty."

"Yeah, I saw her and she wasn't checking you out. She was staring at that un-pierced, virgin skin. I know that look all too well, my friend. How's Shawna?"

"Man, why you always gotta be raggin' on me, dude? Look at her, she's righteous, but she ain't out of my league."

"Look at us, man. She's not only out of our league, but she plays an entirely different sport, my man."

"Pish, posh! Speak for yourself. If you will it, it is no dream."

"What's that?"

"Theodor Herzl, man. If you will it, it is no dream."

"Right, well, 'will' all you want. It ain't happening."

"Have it your way. All I'm saying is … by the way, what are you wearing?"

"I just got off work. I didn't have time to change. Why? Is it that bad?"

"You're wearing a button-up oxford and loafers, and you ask me if it's bad? This isn't the Rotary Club. Let me see that tie," he said, yanking it from my pocket and tying it around my forehead.

"What are you doing? Is this supposed to be cool?"

"No, but at least they won't be looking at your outfit. Plus, you can always say it's some kind of statement against the corporate overlords or something."

"Thanks, man."

"It's nothing, Kev. What can I say? It's a gift. It would be selfish to deny humanity my skills, right?"

"Whatever you … Hey, I think that's Paul," I said, motioning to the silhouette of Paul darkening the shabby door of the club.

As he made his way over, I noticed he lacked his trademark confident gait.

"What it is, fellas? Hey, Donny Rocket," Paul said.

"Hey Paul. Man, I am so glad you are always early," I said.

"Are you sure we should really be here?" Paul asked.

"Well, I don't know if you should be here, pretty boy," Donny taunted.

"You know," Paul groaned. It sounded like a lead-in to a biting comeback, but I knew it wasn't.

"You know" and "don't worry" were Paul's catch-all phrases. They meant a myriad of things from "hello," "goodbye," "stop making fun of me," "I agree," and "how are you, kind sir?" to "Excuse me, I find this *vichyssoise* to be a bit on the runny side."

"Just joking, man. I already have some ladies picked out for us," Donny said.

"Pshht," Paul said, mimicking a walkie-talkie. "Silence radio contact, we are going in. Pshht."

"If Donny's not scared, I'm not," I said, heading out into the writhing abyss of jeans. I tried to make eye contact with some of the girls, but coming up empty just made a beeline for the bar.

"I'll have a Budweiser," I said, leaning the backs of my elbows on top of the bar.

This is where I felt the most comfortable. I've found that it's just exponentially easier to look cool while leaning. Leaning beats standing, kneeling, lying, and squatting hands down when it comes to the "posture coolness" scale. There is no more pathetic feeling than standing in the middle of a room full of people with your shoulders slumped and hands at your sides, while shooting nervous glances at everyone else, as they talk freely and comfortably with one another.

I leaned on the bar for about a half hour, shifting my weight and sipping the beer whenever I needed something to do. The entire time, I was trying to psych myself up to talk to some girl in the vicinity, but to no avail. I would let Paul do the leg work. He had the bait. I would just wait patiently in the boat for the catch. Eventually, my patience paid off.

Paul brought a couple girls over and introduced me to them.

"I want you to meet my friend Kevin. Kevin, this is Stacey and Lily," Paul said coolly.

"Nice to meet you," I said.

This is where I always got stuck. What am I supposed to say to two girls standing in front of me with ripped jeans, intentionally asymmetrical haircuts, and metal studs in their noses? What do I have in common with them?

"You guys know anything about this band?" I finally asked.

"Yeah, they're pretty rad. My brother's friend's cousin is the drummer," said the one I guessed was Stacey.

"Whoa, nice. That's cool," I said.

"Nice outfit, Kevin," the other girl said, flicking the black tie dangling over my ear.

"Oh, this? My stylist says I should wear more black. That's all this is. What do you think? You like it?" I said, striking a pose for her.

"It's slimming," she said.

"Yeah. You don't know the half of it. I'm actually 300 pounds. You can't tell, right?"

"Wow, that's incredible! I never would have guessed. Who's your stylist?"

"His name's Donny, but he's hard to get in to see. He's got a waiting list a mile long. I could probably pull some strings and get you an appointment if you want," I smirked, getting Donny's attention at the end of the bar.

I was about to bring my "A" game, but before I could say, "Did you know Sid Vicious invented the Pogo dance?" or "You know, I was at CBGBs back in the day," the club erupted in a frenzy. Everyone was heading for the door, which was now flooded with flashing red and blue lights.

Somebody yelled above the fray, "It's the fuzz!"

The fire department and police pulled the plug on our joyous evening by declaring the place a fire hazard. Everyone in the club scattered like cockroaches when the light is turned on. The police detained the ones they could and searched them for anything they could find. Paul and I were nineteen years old, and Donny was still eighteen. Because we were in possession of alcoholic beverages, I went to work.

I quickly tucked in my shirt, pulled my wrinkled tie from my head and flung it haphazardly around my neck as we approached the round up.

"These two guys are with me," I said, calmly flashing my Sheriff's Office ID with a big gold star emblazoned on the front. I casually strolled past the cops with my two buddies in tow. In the clear now, we could relax.

"Oh man, I think I need a new pair of pants. See yous! Suckas!" Donny yelled as he vanished into the night, running like a frightened, emaciated ghost, with one hand grasping his jeans to keep them from falling. He was off to soak up more culture.

"See ya, man!" I hollered after him.

Paul and I walked together across the street and sat down in the Sheriff's Office parking lot, watching from afar the lights and commotion of the squad cars, fire trucks, and punkers fleeing the scene.

In the ethereal glow of the flashing reds and blues, we sat and pondered, as we often did, about a different life. A life free from broken-down cars, lousy home lives, low-paying jobs, empty pockets, and second-rate everything. Any life would surely be more satisfying than the one we had. We said nothing, but we both knew what the other was thinking.

Finally, I broke the silence.

"Man, there's got to be something better than this. You know, I would have bought those girls drinks, but I don't have the money. I'm tired of it."

"Isn't there anything you can do? You're supposed to be some kinda genius boy wonder, right? There's gotta be a way."

"Well," I pushed the words out of my mouth, reluctantly at first, "There is something I've been thinking about."

"Yeah?"

"Now, this is just something I've been thinking about, mind you, but there is this account I handle at the Sheriff's Office."

"Uh-huh."

"It's this account that takes deposits for the costs involved in evicting somebody from their house, or office, or whatever. But here's the thing. The account is almost all stale money. Almost all the money in it belongs to dead people, or businesses that moved. And the sheriff doesn't give a rip if these people get their money back because, by law, the money goes into this discretionary account. After ten years, he can do whatever he wants with it; buy squad cars, weapons, boats, whatever, you name it."

"I'm listening. Lay it on me, brother."

For some reason, we automatically started talking in hushed tones.

"Okay. So, let's say I am a Good Samaritan and want to give the money back to these poor slobs who never got their refunds. I would need to cut a check for each and every one of them, and return the money to its rightful owner, right?"

"Yeah, but how would your righteous deeds go unnoticed?"

"Well, listen. Each account only has a small amount of money, say forty, fifty, or sixty bucks, but there are thousands and thousands of them. None of the amounts are enough to arouse any suspicion. It's called salami slicing."

"What about the number of checks?"

"That's the beautiful thing. I handle hundreds of checks every day. I've thought about it. I could slip the bogus checks in with the legit ones and nobody's the wiser."

"Hmm," Paul muttered. I could see his brain processing the odds.

We both sat in silence for several moments, weighing the pros and cons of embarking upon a life of crime. Neither of us really wanted to cross this threshold, but rationalization is a powerful thing.

Life is made up of decisive moments like this. The trouble is, sans the proper road signs, we only see them in hindsight. The way you decide them informs the next set of decisions you will have, and so on, until these decisions either topple over and crush you, or you're standing on top of them with hands raised exultantly.

Joseph Campbell, the famed mythologist, saw the hero's adventure as divided into three sections: *Departure*, *Initiation*, and *Return*. Departure begins with "The Call to Adventure" and "The Crossing of the First Threshold," where the hero is faced with a dilemma outside himself that he must either run from or face. Once he has crossed the first threshold of his adventure, there is no going back.

We were not, of course, heroes in the traditional sense. Actually, we weren't heroes in any sense, but we were being called to cross a threshold by something within ourselves. Something that had been lying in wait in our hearts for a long time. We were sick of being poor, and always having to settle for second best. Why should we not enjoy an effortless and joyful life like so many others around us?

When I was younger, I frequently hung out with two neighborhood guys named Tommy and Jason Tomeleri. Their family was rich, and always rumored to be connected to organized crime. And this, of course, raised their coolness a few notches with all the local kids.

Whenever I would go over to their multilevel house and pass through their laundry room, something always caught my eye. The room was consistently full of loose change from the pants pockets of the family. I would pick the coins off the floor or from the top of the washing machine and pocket them. One day Tommy saw me doing this and screamed, "What are you doing? That's stealing!"

The accusation shocked me. It had never occurred to me that this innocent action could ever be construed as theft. After all, these were just unwanted, stray coins dropped from the pants of people who had enough already and didn't need them. What I was doing was a harmless reallocation or redistribution. It was almost a virtuous, noble, and upright act in my mind. It didn't hurt anybody, but it helped me immensely.

That happened when I was a kid, but here I was proposing a similar kind of crime to Paul.

Finally, Paul piped up. "You're working for *the* Sheriff Nick Navarro, the guy you told me coached Al Pacino how to act like a drug kingpin for the movie, *Scarface*? The guy Chuck Norris calls 'Dad'?" Paul asked rhetorically.

"One and the same."

"And you want to steal from *him*? Mm hmm. I see."

"Yeah, I hear you. Plus, my dad got me this job. I can't screw it up. I really don't see a way to make it happen," I said, already thinking of alternate schemes.

"I'll tell you, though, Navarro is a class-A jerk. He definitely deserves it. One time, he was walking through the office when he just stopped and looked me over. Then he looked at my coworker and said, 'What is *he* doing here? I thought he was just temporary help.'"

"Man. Okay, so the guy's a jerk, but we can't just ...," Paul whispered. I could see the cogs turning in his head. "Well, wait a second. At the bank, I can set up accounts and make deposits into them at will as long as it's within reason. The problem would be, how could you make it seem like all these people were receiving their money?"

"We don't have to. They all kicked the bucket, or they're living 3,000 miles away. I'm telling you, nobody cares about this money. I think we can do this, man. Why not?" I said with hope rising within me.

"This is interesting. Are you sure no one would notice it? Who else besides you takes care of the account?"

"Just me. Only me. I handle everything."

"So, you would print the checks and put them in the pile, right? Who sees them?"

"Just my boss, Laurie. Sometimes she doesn't even look at them. After she signs them, she gives them back and I mail them after work."

"Okay, so you could bring me the checks and I could deposit them."

"How? How do we set up an account?"

"That part is easy. I set up the account as if somebody came in. They would never even question it. We can make withdrawals from the account … actually, accounts, because I think it'd be better to have at least two."

"Who would get the money? Do I have to go in there?"

"No, never. I would take the money out as if a withdrawal was made. It's done all the time."

"I think we can do this. Do you see a down side? How can we get caught? If it gets hairy, we bail. I erase all the accounts we took from and you close the accounts, right?" I said, my excitement growing with the thrill of planning a crime.

Growing up, I always aspired to be an FBI agent. The portrayals of agents in the movies, TV, and comics always looked so cool to me. I would stroll into the place, flash my badge, and tell those local cops to go get a donut because the real pros were here. I would crack that serial killer case by finding some code or pattern in his letters. Cross. Kevin Cross. My name would be in the papers. Maybe they would even make a movie about me.

At age sixteen, I studied my brains out for the FBI entrance exam, but missed by three points. I was crestfallen, but I knew they were looking for lawyers and CPAs, so I decided that would be my focus.

When I graduated high school and left for college, everything seemed possible. I was the boy wonder. I had talent leaking out of my ears. I was an unstoppable force. The world would bow at my greatness. They would talk about how I came from humble beginnings and rose to prominence through sheer genius and force of will. An inspiration to everyone.

But my attempts to get Navarro to notice me were fruitless. When I first discovered the stale accounts, I tried to return the money to their rightful owners, but was scolded for it. Then I had the brilliant idea to take the money and invest it for him. I neglected to tell him this because I knew keeping it secret would make my inevitable announcement that I had made him boatloads of money so much more dramatic:

"Listen, the name's Kevin Cross. Yeah, the guy from accounting. I have been taking that stale money and investing it for you. I doubled it. Yes, you heard right. *Doubled.*"

"Right this way, Mr. Cross. We have a corner office just for you. You're going places, son," Navarro would say. "Johnson, you have one hour to get your filthy junk out of here!"

When he heard of my grand scheme, though, it didn't play out the way it did in my head. He reprimanded me and told me to just do my bleeping job.

"Yes, sir," I responded through clenched teeth.

Here I was, presented with a chance at revenge against Navarro and all the naysayers, along with my perceived enemies living that fast life that I so desperately wanted to be a part of. I would finally rise above the great, unwashed multitude and take hold of my birthright, what was rightfully mine, my divine appointment to greatness.

The plan was perfect. Simple. Elegant. Undetectable.

"What do you think, Paul?"

Paul grinned and said, "You know."

# CHAPTER 2

# pulling it off

I strolled into work the next Monday morning at 8:30 with a renewed sense of purpose. My nerves were on edge, but in a way that just flooded my veins with adrenaline. My mind was eagerly occupied with setting the plan in motion, but I couldn't let on that anything was different.

"Hey Melvin, how you doing?" I said, nodding to the front desk officer as he buzzed me in.

"Ahh, same old, same old," Melvin replied.

"Yep, I hear ya. Same here," I answered, heading to my desk.

"Hey, Kev, whaddya do this weekend?" I heard from behind me.

It was Shelly, a woman who once was very athletic but had not darkened the door of a gym in several years. She hated men, but always seemed to be involved in the worst sort of business with them. She had been around the block a few times and even lapped some of the other girls there. Her exploits became the fodder for all kinds of crude office humor and were always well played out among the Civil Division's thirty employees.

"Oh, nothing really. You?" As soon as the words escaped my mouth, I regretted them. I knew I didn't want to know the answer if I wanted to eat lunch later. Luckily, my boss Laurie Sanders was walking by at that very moment.

"Shelly, would you be kind enough to see me in my office?" Laurie asked, placing a gentle hand on Shelly's shoulder.

"I'll be right there. See you, Kev," Shelly replied.

Laurie Sanders was a striking woman of average height and shoulder length, dirty blond hair, which she meticulously styled to almost resemble a helmet. And that, coupled with her perpetually downturned lips, gave her a stern countenance; a look at complete odds with her pleasant personality. She was very professional and cordial, and commanded the respect of everyone, but never got close to or joked with anyone in the office.

Like most days, I saw my dad talking to his boys, the fellow civil deputies: Gus Dimico, Jerry Williams, Vince Giordano, Kevin Moran, and Mr. Berkowitz, who was a volunteer but still part of the inner circle. My dad's gig was a cushy retirement job, one highly coveted by everyone in law enforcement, and one that many had only reached by virtue of knowing the right people. Many of the boys would meet at Lester's Diner and talk war stories over coffee before serving their twenty or so subpoenas for the day. My dad consistently served more than the rest of the guys. Somehow he never understood that his job was always secure as long as he drew breath.

For that matter, even in death he could still draw a paycheck, or so went the oft-circulated story of Old Lou. He was a former hard-nose bailiff, whom no one had seen in months. His desk sat empty, his box overflowing with unserved subpoenas. Every month, Old Lou's salary was direct deposited into his account and apparently used, though no one knew for sure if Lou was dead or alive.

I nodded to the boys and made my way to the bookkeeping and accounting corner of the Civil Division. The Sheriff's Office was straight out of *Serpico*: a big open, warehouse-style space with old, uniform desks lined up in rows. I'm convinced that every office from that era ordered their furniture and filing cabinets out of the same catalog, whose mission, apparently, was to slowly deaden the spirit of the worker.

Every desk was covered in horrible faux-wood paneling with a row of metallic drawers on one side, and a space for a similarly depressing chair on the other. On each desk sat one dot matrix printer, one industrial sized stapler, a pen receptacle, and an "in-out" file bin. Everything was old, stale, and dusty; a description that aptly fit most of the employees inhabiting the space. Mercifully, after awhile, the screeching cacophony of dot matrix printers almost became a relaxing white noise, like one of those bedside radios with soothing sea sounds or forest ambience.

I was a tender nineteen years old and this was just my first stop on a long and illustrious career in law enforcement, so I happily trudged through this dank environment day in and day out.

"Gooood Morning, Phyllis Carbo! Have a good weekend?" I said, putting on my usual jovial affect.

"Oh, so-so. I had to take little Fupsy to the vet on Saturday because the poor little thing was sick."

Phyllis Carbonetta was one of those people who thought of her pets as children, and shared their every exploit with anyone within earshot. When they stopped listening, she would just talk out loud to herself with seemingly no awareness of this fact.

As the Civil Division assistant bookkeeper, she sat directly across from me. A position far enough to have sufficient autonomy, but close enough for a great vantage point to observe her every idiosyncrasy.

I called her Phyllis Carbo because of the striking resemblance she bore to Greta Garbo. She was what Greta Garbo in her prime would look like thirty years older and thirty pounds heavier. Every month she religiously went to the barber and asked for a boy's bowl haircut to go with her frumpy boy's clothes. Phyllis's quirks, though, were the lovable kind, and they only served to endear her more to everyone around her. She took a particular liking to me, and always defended and cared for me.

"Oh, I'm so sorry to hear that. Is he okay now?" I asked.

"Yeah, I'm giving him antibiotics every four hours. Of course, I won't be there today, so I asked my neighbor to do it for me. She's a sweetheart. She has two poodles herself, so she knows what a job it is to take care of them. Until you have one, you can't understand how it is, really. Do you have any?"

"Well, my parents weren't what you would call 'animal people,' you know? I did have a stray cat named Flash when I was young …"

"Because you can't even imagine what Fupsy does when I am away. He misses his little mommy wommy. He waits by the door sometimes all day until I get back. It's the cutest thing to see him waiting there with those big puppy wuppy eyes. Did I show you the pictures of him?"

"I think so. Once or twice," I said, trying to disguise my hesitance in having to look at the photos of Fupsy and her other dog Conner for the umpteenth time.

"Well, they're the cutest things. If you saw them, you would want to mash their little cheeks."

"Oh, I'm sure. Hey, what's on the docket today?" I knew what I had to do, but I needed to redirect the conversation fast.

As Phyllis began to run down the list of tasks, my mind wandered to the real task at hand. I flicked on the computer and began to look through the database titled "Suspense Accounts."

When a person in Broward County wanted to evict someone from an office or apartment, they had to put down a deposit to cover all the anticipated costs of the eviction, such as locks, letters, storage, etc. The deposit was always an even amount of somewhere between $100 and $500, but the actual costs for each eviction varied, so there was usually something left over.

The Sheriff's Office had no interest in paying someone to give the person back their $10 because it wasn't worth the hassle. After ten years the money automatically went into the Sheriff's account to use for whatever he saw fit. The amounts were too small for anyone to complain about, and usually the owners were so happy to have the person evicted that the leftover chump change was the last of their concerns.

My job entailed handling all the accounts payable for any account related to the Civil Division. Every month, it was my personal charge to balance these "suspense accounts." The record of every transaction was saved on large hard drives, which looked like oversized floppy drives, and stored in a password-protected safe. I and another guy in the office were the only ones who knew the password to this safe.

On a monthly basis, I balanced the account and printed out a 1,000-page report, which I gave two people for approval: Luis Quintana, the CFO and close friend of Nick Navarro, and Lloyd, the internal auditor.

Lloyd was a jovial, grandfatherly type who must have been in his late sixties. His receding hairline formed a soft "W" on his head that he occasionally buzzed, leaving his white hair too short to comb, and sticking a half-inch straight up and out. His abnormally long earlobes swung a little bit whenever he moved his head. He was a company man who was on his way to retirement and enjoyed being a mentor to the younger workers at the Civil Division. He took to me quickly and got a real rise out of calling me "young buck," "boy wonder," and a myriad of other things.

Obviously, Lloyd and Luis couldn't look through the entire thousand pages, and so they just focused on the recently active accounts. I figured I would start with the oldest accounts first. Some were several years old and not one had asked for their money back, so I thought they were perfectly safe.

I scrolled down to the oldest stale accounts: Cesar Garcia—$27.98, Jerry Gaddon—$39.54, Rosenberg, Cohen and Cohen—$73.17, Layton Accounting Associates—$168.56. As my eyes scanned the list, my blood started to race. There were literally thousands of small accounts like this. It was ghost money, up for grabs. *I should be rewarded for my ingenuity*, I thought. *This is genius.*

I was startled out of my focus by Phyllis.

"Where did I put that? Oh, here it is," she muttered to herself, or maybe for the benefit of everybody around.

While I wish I could lay claim to this brilliant scheme I was putting into motion, the idea was not entirely mine, but was inspired by a phone call several months before:

"Kevin Cross, Civil Division."

"Ah, yeah, this is Barry Fenning. I don't know if you're the right guy to talk to. I was told you handle the stale monies account there."

"Yeah, that's me. What can I do for you?"

"Okay, great. You see, I'm a private investigator. I was wondering, this is just a question, mind you, but I was wondering if there would be any way to get the names and addresses of the folks that are due a refund. I am interested in returning this money, you understand. Now, I have done this sort of thing before and it usually works like this: you simply provide me with the names, and for finding the people and giving them their refund, I take a fifty percent fee. How does that ..."

"Well, honestly, I'm not sure I'm allowed to give you that kind of information."

"It's Kevin, right?"

"Kevin. Yeah."

"Okay, Kevin. I'm in a particular position in which I am prepared to give you ten percent of my fifty percent fee. Now, that's ten percent of everything for just providing the information, mind you. You don't have to do anything, you understand."

"I have been trying to return the money to these people. I've been going through all the accounts and I've already sent out a few hundred checks, but a heck of a lot of them come back."

"That's where I come in. You just have addresses, but I find people. It's what I do, you know?"

"You sure this is completely above board?"

"Absolutely. This kind of thing is done all the time. I just want to see these people get the money they deserve."

"I'll tell you what. I'll give you some names to start, but I don't want any money. Whatever you charge is fine."

I gave the guy about $50,000 worth of accounts, but the little seed had been planted in my head. As more and more checks came back undeliverable, what was previously unclear was now obvious. This was phantom money for phantom people.

About a month into this, the Sheriff caught wind of my little agreement with the P.I. Although what we were doing was legal, he wasn't interested in spending resources trying to get money back to people who had all but forgotten they were even owed. Navarro told us to shut it down, so I called the guy and told him it was off.

This whole business was a slippery slope, though, and once I put one foot on the incline, it wasn't long before I was sliding full hurdle.

I started with accounts that were so stale they were rancid, but I wanted to make sure there was no way they would call in six months looking for their refund. I looked up the names and businesses in the Dade and Broward County Yellow Pages, and called 411 on the Sheriff's dime to make sure they had shut their doors or moved away.

When I had assured myself that the coast was clear, I got right down to business. Laurie Sanders, my immediate boss, signed off on the checks every day and there was no reason for her to not trust me. She was getting ready to retire and already had a foot out the door. Nothing about the names or checks would give her pause.

I thought it best to stay on the safe side anyway. I decided the first week would be a test. I would use the dilution method: mix ten or twenty bogus checks in with a hundred or so legitimate checks. By doing this, even if we got audited, the chances of a phony check coming up in a random sample were next to nothing.

It always struck me as an odd thing, but all the attention at the Sheriff's Office was focused on accounts receivable. Audits happened every year and Phyllis had to reconcile every account by the end of every day.

Because of this, a firestorm of activity invariably swirled around her desk, while I, the sole person entirely in charge of accounts payable, was left virtually undisturbed. The temptation was extraordinary because I controlled the means to completely cover my own tracks. Within my basic job duties lay the tools to steal vast amounts of money and erase all evidence of it ever having existed. For my impoverished yet agile nineteen-year-old mind, it was all too much to ignore.

I went back to my real work for a little bit, ruminating over the next step, and engaging in one of my favorite pastimes: sneaking glances at Amber, the cutest girl at the Sheriff's Office. She was a stunning brunette and the daughter of the Chief of Police, which made her dangerous, yet enticing at the same time. *Someday, I will ask her out*, I thought.

Before I knew it, lunchtime was upon me.

"You ready, Kev?" I heard a voice say.

Oh, yeah. I forgot I had told Carolyn I would have lunch with her. Carolyn was a slender, tall woman in her early thirties, with long brown hair tied back in a braided ponytail. She wore oversized, artisan-made earrings that complimented her round face. Carolyn always brought her own lunch and walked to work every day. She constantly extolled the virtues of frugality to me, but it seemed strange to purposely deprive yourself of things you could be enjoying right now. She was also probably the only person in the office free of any annoying eccentricities, so I always welcomed the respite.

"Oh, I can't believe it," I said. "I knew I forgot something. I promise you, I made a lunch, but it is sitting on my kitchen counter."

"It's okay, I'm prepared. I brought a little more today, and besides, we can share," Carolyn said in her singsong way.

"I couldn't do that to you. Really, it's okay. I can buy a lunch."

"No, no. I insist. C'mon."

We proceeded to split everything from her lunch bag, an act which I found a little embarrassing, since all the things in her little brown sack struck me as pathetic. They were off-brand, ugly, mashed-up items that were almost unrecognizable.

Because I was raised in poverty, my mom always tried to make things stretch. She bought the cheapest stuff from the dirty grocery store, where every can was either dented or a cheap imitation of the name brand items. All the poor people shopped there. Even as a kid I sensed that everyone who shopped there was acutely conscious of this fact, and I was keenly aware of the shame on their faces, and my own. They avoided eye contact and would talk in hushed tones, sometimes even whispering. I, too, kept my head lowered, staring at the ground, trying to keep a low profile in case anyone from school saw me clutching a box of "Fruity O's" or a piece of bruised fruit.

So, it made me more than a little uncomfortable to see Carolyn pulling all these pitiful items from her little bag, and displaying them for the world to see. It was the very thing I was running from—the feeling of shame at the inadequacy of my possessions in the eyes of others. I yearned to have the things which automatically demanded respect from the world, and the homemade bologna sandwich she had made was not on that list.

"I have to ask. Why are you sharing your lunch with me when I could just buy one?" I inquired, unfolding the plastic flap on my sandwich bag.

"Well, I guess I didn't really think about it. I think my mom raised me this way. I know it sounds cheesy, but it gives me a little shot of happiness to do things for people, even little things."

"Really?"

"Sure. I don't know why exactly, but it does. This job gives me enough money to do what I want in life, and I really don't have much stress. I've never been the kind of person who yearns for stuff. I'm not a yearner," she said, pushing a little chocolate cake wrapped in plastic across the table to me. "I've found, for me, that being content with what I have is the secret to happiness."

"Easy for you to say. You didn't grow up poor."

"You'd be surprised. I've been both rich and poor. It may sound strange coming from me, but money and possessions, and all that stuff, don't do that much for you. You study any philosophy in school?"

"A little bit," I lied.

"Well, there's this quote I love from a famous philosopher. He was a guy from Denmark by the name of Kierkegaard. I don't remember where I saw it, but it's always stuck with me."

I was a little shocked by Carolyn's intelligence. She had never revealed herself this way before.

"It goes sort of like this. Money and possessions are like a wolf in sheep's clothing. They pretend to be protecting you from anxiety and pain, but they really eventually become the source of anxiety and pain. They protect you as well as a wolf would protect the sheep from wolves."

"Hmm," I said through a mouthful of chocolate.

When I got back to my desk, Phyllis was still gone, so I had some time to crunch the numbers. I added together the stalest seventeen accounts and hit "enter." Grabbing a blank check, I put it in my printer and watched as the numbers slowly, line by line, appeared before my eyes with each pass of the ribbon. Seventy-three-dollars-and-seventeen-cents. I sat there staring at the figure for what seemed like an eternity.

"Huh. Shouldn't have eaten that last one," Phyllis said to herself. She had returned to see me staring blankly at my printer, but must have thought nothing of it.

I pulled the check out of the printer and set it on my desk.

*There it is. I did it. It's done now*, I told myself.

And it was easy. Nothing to it, really. I immediately started dreaming of the things I would buy with it. This was easy, because my head was constantly filled with an ever-burgeoning list of things I wanted or needed. Actually, in my mind the money was spent after the second or third item on the list.

Obviously, this paltry amount wouldn't do. Before the day was up, I printed seventeen more checks, working my way up the list of stale accounts. *A couple grand should be enough to last us for a few months*, I thought. We would be careful with it. Save it and invest it. Buy things for our families. Maybe a couple things for me, but nothing too crazy.

At the end of the day, I took my checks and mixed some of them in randomly with the stack of authentic checks for the day. Every day I had to get the checks to Laurie for her to sign, approve, and return for me to mail. I figured I could sneak a few checks in every day and have them all approved by the end of the week.

Luckily, Laurie was on the phone when I poked my head into her office. If I was behaving any differently, she wouldn't notice. I simply motioned with my hand that I was bringing the checks to her and set them on the desk. She gave me the cursory nod of the head to indicate "message received."

Even though I knew I was more likely to be abducted by aliens than be discovered, I was still preoccupied with this for the rest of the day. What if I did something wrong? Maybe there was something I didn't think about. Maybe she would catch some difference in the checks that I couldn't foresee. I plugged away at my work for the rest of the afternoon in this manner, barely concentrating on what I was doing.

"Mr. Cross, here you go," Laurie said, dropping a stack of signed checks on my desk several hours later.

"Oh, thanks," I said, snapping out of my trance.

I casually flipped through the checks to see if mine were kosher. There they were. Checks made out to two different fake names that Paul and I decided on, Ira Cohen and Raul Cinfuentes.

It was the summer of 1986, and since we were both big *Miami Vice* fans, it seemed fitting to cull the names directly from the show. It played perfectly into this whole fantasy world we were creating of clandestine meetings, genius schemes, and covert operations.

After I left work that day, I mailed the legit checks and stuck the misappropriated checks in my front pocket, patting them cheerfully. That night I would meet Paul at a bar, give him the checks, and toast our new-found fortune.

When I entered the bar, Paul was already there.

"Yo, yo, little brother, you gonna get it from your dad and your mother. What it is?" I greeted him with the lyrics to a cheesy 80s pop song.

"My brotha from another motha. What it is, what it is?" Paul answered, giving me the requisite "high-five." In those days, the high-five had not evolved to the level it has reached today. It was a simple slap of the palms. The only variation came when you moved your hands up high, down low, or around the back.

"Oh, you know, kickin' tires, lighting fires."

"So? Enough with the formalities. Howdit go?"

"Well, I have good news and bad news. What do you want to hear first?" I asked.

"Um, gimme the bad news."

"Okay, listen. The bad news is they caught me today. I was printing the checks and they just caught me. I got fired."

"Right," Paul said, rolling his eyes. "And the good news?"

"The good news is I'm not going to prison. I plea-bargained and gave you up to the fuzz, so only you are going to jail. How's that for good news, my compadre?"

"Hilarious. But really. Do you have them?"

"Read 'em and weep," I said, pulling the folded checks from my pocket and slapping them down on the table.

"Let me see this!" Paul barked with delight, barely containing himself. "Choice! Raul Cinfuentes, Ira Cohen! This is so 'Vice'! This is incredible, Kev."

"I know. I know. It was easy as cake, my man. E-Z."

"Same on my end. Everything is totally kosher. I set up the two accounts, no prob. I will deposit them tomorrow and we will have the money by Friday."

"Oh, and there's something else I forgot to tell you. I have a perfect excuse for why I would be printing so many refund checks. A couple months ago this P.I. called and wanting to find people and give the money back, so I told him 'yeah.' Plus I've given hundreds of refunds, so the secret's out. I can just say, 'Sorry, but listen, I let the cat out of the bag by accident and there's gonna be people asking for refunds, but I'm not actively telling people they have money.'"

"You are the man, Kevin Cross."

"How can I be the man if you're the man?"

"Four letters for you: M-I-N-O. MINO, baby!"

"MINO."

M.I.N.O. was an acronym popular within our circle that meant "Money Is No Object." We often used it jokingly because of our impoverished states, but it would soon take on a new life and become a motto, or mantra of sorts.

We finished off our night of ill-conceived celebration by drinking ourselves senseless, and through some miracle, drove home safely.

The next few days at work were tense as I constantly felt the impending doom, the other shoe ready to fall on me. At any moment, I was expecting a tap on the shoulder and a voice to say, "Can you step into my office, Kevin?" I was trying harder than ever to keep up appearances as the jovial, honest, up-and-coming Kevin Cross. The sweet young kid, the hard worker, the trustworthy employee. Move along folks, nothing to see here.

After several days of normalcy, my confidence began to grow in our scheme and my abilities. I could trust in myself. I knew that now. My own ingenuity and talents would lead me to true happiness and could rescue me from any situation.

The money cleared into the accounts of Mr. Cinfuentes and Mr. Cohen, and subsequently to those of Mr. Cross and Mr. Johnson. The take for the first week equaled out to a couple thousand bucks, which for Paul and me was a windfall of major proportions.

MINO, baby.

# CHAPTER 3

# addicted to money

Maybe it was because it was the first take. Or maybe it was because this desire had been lying dormant in me, growing and waiting for the opportunity to finally stretch its legs. When I gave it an opening, it finally erupted forth, and all the money was spent within the first two or three days after clearing the account. My plans to invest and save wisely all evaporated in a brief moment at the prospect of buying top shelf liquor at the chicest restaurants in Miami, getting a Pioneer tape player and sound system, and souping up my Saab 900S.

The white Saab 900S was the possession around which my existence revolved. When I was in high school, I was bitten by a dog at a junk yard where I was looking for a gear shifter end. My friend Donny had thrown mine out the window, pretending that it was a grenade and we were in some kind of James Bond movie. All I found at the junk yard was a rabid, mangy, and underfed dog who used my leg as a quick meal. I won a $7,000 settlement and used the money to buy a Saab, even though my dad urged me to invest it, or at least buy a new car on the market called an Acura Integra, which I would probably still own today.

I rejected my dad's wisdom, and it thus became my life's work to upgrade and fix my beloved beast of a Saab 900S. The first lucre from our dirty scheme went almost exclusively to the maintenance of the White Demon.

Spending the money felt so surreal. This was Monopoly money, and it meant nothing whatsoever to me. It flew through my hands with disgusting ease. There was no feeling of remorse, like when I spent my own money. When you spend money that you have earned, it feels as if you are losing a part of yourself, which gives you that all-important internal monologue of "Should I buy this, or shouldn't I?" When you work for something, its value becomes easier to appreciate.

This phony cash was different. I had no regrets at all, and let me tell you, it felt amazing. When you buy something you desire, it literally spikes your blood with a potent cocktail of adrenaline and endorphins, releasing precious doses of serotonin into your body, making you feel warm and fuzzy inside. Forget what everybody says, buying stuff is ridiculously satisfying.

But, there are several problems with this type of satisfaction. One, it wears off with alarming quickness, and two, the rush diminishes with time and repetition. This produces the unfortunate dilemma of having to go back to the source with ever-increasing frequency, or increasing the dose as the feeling progressively wanes.

These first times, though, I felt that fantastic, glorious surge of joy through my veins and rejoiced in the feeling. Everything just felt right.

Although I was raised in a Christian household and went to Christian school most of my life, I adhered to many philosophies at complete odds with my upbringing. The Christianity I knew was simply unequipped to handle the modern dilemmas that I was facing. So I turned to others to supplement the places where I found it lacking.

*De Consolatione Philosophiae*, the philosophical work that laid the groundwork for much of medieval thought, had as its central concept the idea of the *Rota Fortunae*, or "Wheel of Fortune." Boethius, the Roman, who wrote *Consolatione* while unjustly imprisoned, said that a blind goddess spins us on a wheel of fortune and that our luck comes in cycles, undisturbed by our religions, ideologies, or philosophies. Sometimes I felt as if I was just on the beginning of a good spin. The good Goddess Fortuna was shining upon me. My lucky cycle had begun.

All these things were beyond my control. I was inextricably tied to this wheel which contained my destiny, and was helpless to attempt to act against it. I didn't think about it in these terms at the time, but this was essentially how I was living.

I also derived much of my attitude about life from the theory of evolution. After all, if evolution is true, it answers the most fundamental question that man has been asking for millennia: "Why are we here?"

I believed that we are here because organisms produce more offspring than can survive, and these offspring vary in their capacity to survive and reproduce. We are here, I believed, because of an indiscriminate force working in nature that randomly prizes one trait over another. We are sentient, thanks to a series of fortunate attributes fitting our environment at the right time. According to some theories of evolution, life becomes smarter, faster, and better, as a result of the competition for food and suitable mates. One trait develops through a mutation, or is slowly passed from parent to child in gradual degrees, based on the way that trait is suited for its environment.

If there is no moral system or hand guiding this grand movement of life, only suitability and non-suitability, then it is no great mental leap to convince yourself that you are simply acting to be the fittest by any means necessary. This was just the simple reality of life as I saw it.

I don't think I ever thought about what I was doing on this level, but this incorrect thinking was certainly acting on me subconsciously as I rationalized my actions. The gluttonous, "greed is good" attitude of the 1980s only threw fuel on this uncontrollable fire.

The first test worked so well, and the two of us spent the money with such remarkable speed, that it was soon time to dip into the well once again. But first, I had to prepare the end of the month report and balance the suspense account.

"Hey Phyllis!" I greeted my fellow employee with a genuine grin.

"Well, you are very chipper this morning, Kevin," she replied.

"Well, can you blame me? Sitting across from a babe like you every day?"

"Ohhhh myyyy. Flattery will get you everywhere with me," she chirped, swiveling around in her chair to look at me and gauge my sincerity.

"Really? Well, that's what I was going for," I said. "How are you doing today, Ms. Carbo?"

"Oh, I'm good. Same old, same old. You know, this place would fall apart without me. This place will suck it right outta ya. Don't let 'em do it to you. You're still young. You've got the, uh, what do they call it again? Oh yeah, hope," Phyllis said, giggling at her own wittiness.

"Okay, Ms. Carbo, I'll make sure that doesn't happen." If she only knew how much I was making sure.

"Did you hear about Shelly? Oh, mama. Listen to this. You will never believe who she's dating."

"Honestly, I'd rather not …"

"Cesar from the janitor crew," she continued, "I know, it's crazy! You know that guy. The one with the lazy eye. I think it's a lazy eye. I'm not sure. What do you call that when one of the eyes is looking in another direction? You know? You don't know which one to look at. Which one is he seeing me with? I think the best way is just to pretend you are doing something when you're talking to them. I just don't want to be rude, you know?"

"Yeah, I know. But really, I don't need to hear any more details about Shelly. I like her and I want to keep it that way," I said, trying to end the conversation there.

"Okay, Mr. Party Pooper. Somebody's got a case of the Mondays. Whatcha got today?"

"Well, it's that time of month again. I have to balance the suspense account."

"Already? Wow. Well, I'll tell ya, time flies," she said.

"Sure does. You are right about that," I said, turning my attention to balancing the numbers.

I had to change the balance to zero on the accounts that I had pilfered from, to make it seem as if the people had been given a refund. I would put a note on the account to denote that it had been refunded, but no one would ever see it. When I handed over this mammoth, thousand-page report every month, no one in their right mind would rifle through to the last entries. No one really cared enough, and nobody had the time to be that meticulous. As long as everything balanced, no one ever bothered to look any closer.

I hurriedly got to work covering my tracks, but it was difficult because my office crush, Amber, was within my clear line of sight. Sometimes I would think she was sneaking glances at me, but she was far enough away that it was hard to tell. I didn't want to linger too long because that's creepy, but I imagined that she was ogling me, casting flirty looks in my direction.

I think the sudden influx of money did something to my ego. I sat there for a moment, summoning the courage to get up and go talk to her. I rose from my chair with alpha male gusto, accidentally thrusting my chair backwards into another desk with an audible thud. No one seemed to notice.

I strolled over to her desk in a casual, jerking walk which I imagined was just dripping with subtle confidence and sexiness. She would be putty in my hands.

With each step, though, my confidence waned. Before I knew it, I was standing in front of her.

"What's up, Kevin?" Amber chirped.

"Ahh, well, umm, I, uh, just wanted to ...," I stammered.

"Hey, girl," Shelly chimed in from behind me. "You have a killer weekend?" Amber was great friends with Shelly, although she was the polar opposite of Shelly in terms of men. Amber was sweet and pure, and seemingly very innocent, so it always seemed strange to me to see such a friendship blossom.

"Oh, not really. Didn't really do anything. There was an *I Love Lucy* marathon on and I just couldn't break away. They showed the one where she's crushing grapes in Italy to impress the Italian director. Did you see that one?"

"Of course, girl. That's a classic," she said, laughing out loud and trying out her best Lucy impression, while holding her pants up and prancing around in a circle as if she were crushing grapes.

"You are too funny!" Amber said, putting a hand over her mouth to suppress her laughter. People were starting to look.

"Oh, hey, Kev!" Shelly said, finally acknowledging my presence. "I'm doing Lucy crushing the grapes. You know, the one where she's crushing grapes. Watch this." I must have inspired her to do an encore because she proceeded to demonstrate her impression again for my benefit.

"Oh, yeah, that's a good one. My mom watches that show all the time," I said. "What it is, Shelly?"

"Ahhhh, you know. Same stuff, different day. What are you doing over here?"

"Oh, nothing. Just saying 'Hi' to Amber. So, 'Hi Amber'," I said.

"Hi, Kevin," Amber answered sweetly.

"Soooooo, I better get back to work or I'm gonna be here late tonight," I said, easing backwards a few steps.

"Ok, well, I'll see you later, okay?" Amber said.

"Yeah, see ya, Kev," Shelly added.

"Bye, you two."

I turned and headed back to my chair, defeated.

I set my mind back to working on the report and plugged away without getting up for several hours. At the end of the day, with everything balanced, I set the oversized dot matrix to printing. This printer was so large it had its own desk next to mine and was fed by huge boxes of 11x14-sized non-perforated paper so I could bind them easily. The printing was an all-night procedure, so when I came in the next morning, the report would be ready to be bound and handed in to Lloyd and Luis.

I arrived home to the smell of my mother cooking something. My mom loved to cook and spent long hours in the kitchen preparing grand meals for her family. Her favorite ingredient, which she used to great effect, was garlic. The woman could subsist solely on the stuff. Anything and everything was immediately rendered edible by sprinkling a little garlic on it. As a result, the lingering smell of garlic always hung around the house. We were all used to it, but when people came over they always thought something was cooking. They were usually right.

My mother and father moved to Hollywood, Florida, from Philadelphia when I was three years old and bought a house on Tyler Street, a beautiful road lined with enormous royal palm trees on either side. The house was an old Spanish-style abode and had a big steeple-looking chimney in the front that made it look a little like a small village's church in South America. It was situated just three blocks from Hollywood Beach and Florida Bible Christian School, where I attended most of my life.

My mother had an aversion to public schools, and for good reason. The private school I went to was as bad as the public schools when it came to behavior. I learned my first curse words, drank my first drink, and did drugs for the first time, all with kids from the Christian school. I think this behavior stems from overreacting to the "nerd" stigma that comes with going to a private or Christian school. The kids from public school looked down on the private school kids, and so we always had to prove we were capable of committing the same sins that they were doing to cast off this nagging feeling of inadequacy.

Florida Bible was no different. I met Tommy and Jason Tomeleri there; two brothers who moved down from New York with their mother when she divorced their father and changed the family name from Brognoli to Tomeleri. Jason was the studious one of the two. He had aspirations of becoming a lawyer, and his nose was constantly buried in a law book.

Tommy's life, on the other hand, focused almost exclusively on partying and girls. He was extremely gregarious and fancied himself an athlete and a ladies' man, but was awarded the nickname "Fat Boy," thanks to the pudgy stomach always protruding from under his skin-tight shirts. Tommy and Jason's personalities were more than evident even at ten years of age when they moved into the neighborhood, and their family settled into one of the larger houses in the community, a fact which did not go unnoticed by anyone.

Tommy was known for asking everybody one of two things: "Hey man, you wanna smoke a doobie?" and "Bro, when are gonna set me up with somebody? You got any girls for me?"

The answers were usually "yes" to the first account and "no" to the second.

Tommy and Jason hung out with another neighborhood guy named Charlie Moreno. Charlie and the brothers Tomeleri, especially Tommy, were inseparable. I saw Charlie in the halls of my high school and occasionally with Tommy and Jason, but I knew him mostly by his reputation as a playboy. He drove a Porsche, wore tailored Armani suits, $50 socks and Pismo Beach loafers, and lived in an exclusive gated community. The exaggerated stories that circulated around the community about his many exploits with women became legendary.

I walked in the kitchen and greeted my mom with a big kiss on her cheek.

"Hey, Ma. What're you cooking?" I asked.

"Oh, just a little spaghetti. How are you? How was work?"

"Just fine."

"Are you eating okay? You look too skinny. Look at you. Are you eating enough at work? Because I don't think you are eating enough at work."

"I'm eating enough at work, Ma. Listen, I'm thinking of becoming a vegetarian," I said casually, reveling in the shock I knew this would create.

"*What?* Why?" she asked, putting down the knife she was chopping with. "What would you do that for? You are skinny enough as it is."

"Well, it's healthier for one thing. That red meat is terrible for you, don't you know that?"

"Bah, everything they say is bad for you is actually good for you. You know what's bad for you is all that fake stuff you get from that health place. You know I don't use anything fake. Not one thing. Real butter, real milk, real everything, and look at me. I'm healthy as anybody on this planet. What would you want to stop eating meat for? God put cows here for a reason," she said, wiping her hands on her apron.

"Not all meat. Just red meat and chicken. I'm still gonna eat fish."

"And I have the money to feed you fish every night? Where do you think you are, Europe? While you're in *my* house, we eat meat."

"Okay, have it your way. Is Cindy here?" I asked, changing the subject, satisfied with the reaction I got.

"I don't think so. She's still at work," she said, still eying me suspiciously.

My sister, Cindy, was a cop for the Hollywood Police Department, and she used to use me in some of her sting operations. She sometimes was in charge of busting bars for serving alcohol to minors, so she would send me into these bars and I would ask for alcohol. If they served me, I would leave and my sister would bust in and serve them with a fine. I never got to drink the alcohol, but learning the names of all the drinks and which bars would serve you, if you were underage, contributed greatly to my delinquency.

The information was like gold in high school. I would dole it out to the most deserving candidates, namely, girls I liked and guys I wanted to be friends with. It upped my "cool" factor tenfold to be able to casually say, "Yeah, you know G's over on US1? They serve me alcohol all the time."

"Well, I'll be in my room if you need me. Love ya, Ma," I said.

"Give me a kiss," she said, turning her head and pushing her cheek out expectantly.

In my room I turned on the TV and called Paul.

"Hey par'ner, what it is?" I said. "How you doing?"

"Good, good, good. Hey, guess who I saw?" Paul asked rhetorically. "Your girl, Cathy Winarski."

"Stugotz! Did she say anything about me?"

"Nope. She was with one-armed Tony."

One-armed Tony was thusly named due to a leather jacket he always wore on just one arm, so that the other sleeve hung limply like a phantom limb. He was pierced and tattooed in every possible place, and was famous in our circle for being the most hardcore guy we knew. Cathy Winarski dated one-armed Tony periodically, but I was forever trying to convince her that this was a mistake. This was a Herculean task because she spent all her time with one-armed Tony. Whenever I was lucky enough to catch her alone, I would offer up for her a list of pros and cons. Mostly pros about dating me and cons about dating one-armed Tony.

"Look at you. You are too beautiful to waste your time with him," I would say. "One-armed Tony has no future. I do. I am already in college and I work for the Sheriff."

This almost worked sometimes. I could see in her eyes that my arguments for the plaintiff were beginning to convince her, but then one-armed Tony would get her back in his clutches. Or "clutch" on account of the one-armed thing.

As we continued our phone conversation, I hoped that Paul had tried to match us up. "You put in a good word for me?" I asked.

"No way, man, I told her you were a big loser and one-armed Tony was the man. I said she'd be crazy not to marry him. Do you, one-armed Tony, take Cathy Winarski to be your lawfully wedded wife? To have and to …"

"Funny. Thanks for looking out. Listen, how are you on money?"

"Broke again. When are we making another withdrawal for Mr. Cohen?"

"Soon, my friend. Mañana I turn in a report for that account and then we will be golden for another month. They put it all on these giant hard drives and I rotate them so there is never a backup older than a day. When I delete one of the accounts and make a backup over it, it's gone for good."

"Let's do it. Everything is roses on my end."

"I already have some targets for next time. I'll be able to do it this week. What are we doing this weekend?" I asked.

"I don't know. You want to go to City Limits?"

"Who's playing?"

"Who knows? But it's the best place in Fort Lauderdale."

"Yeah, you're right. They always accept my fake ID there. Sometimes they don't even check it. All right, let's go, buddy."

"Cool. I'll call you later this week. We should go to the health store and get some supplements too. I'll give you a call."

⇒

When I came into to work the next day, I bound the printed report and hauled it over to Fredys' office. Fredys' assistant, Phyllis, always took the report from me to give to her boss, but I suspected that she probably just looked it over herself and gave the approval without Luis even glancing at it. He had bigger fish to fry than balancing the suspense accounts. That suited me just fine.

Phyllis was on the phone when I gave her the report, so we just nodded to one another knowingly. Honestly, I planned it this way. Sometimes I would wait until the person I needed to see was busy with something else, and then I'd just slip in and out virtually unnoticed.

Like clockwork, Phyllis returned with the approved report a little while later and we exchanged shallow pleasantries.

Next was Lloyd, the internal auditor. Eager to finish the job, I immediately took the report to him.

"Hey, Lloyd, how are you doing today?"

"Well, young buck. What do you have for me?"

"Just the report for the suspense accounts."

"That time again, huh? Boy, oh boy," he said, shaking his head and pursing his lips. "You know, they say life is what happens when you're busy doing something else."

Lloyd's speech-making and philosophizing were legendary around the office. He was given to long-windedness, even when you had already heard one of his lectures. "Be careful, son. Don't let life slip by while you are busy making plans. I'll tell you this; life doesn't care about your plans. You know, I wanted to be travel writer when I was younger. Can you believe that? There was no such thing as a travel writer, you know?"

"No kidding?"

"Yes siree. You know I ran away from home when I was four?"

I did, but I didn't stop him.

"They picked me up a few blocks away, dragging my suitcase down a dirt road. Another time, I took off, I was about eleven

42

then. I took off, went to the bus station and rode the bus until the end. Two o'clock in the morning, I'm sitting around in the bus station when a cop comes over and he says to me, he says, 'Who're you waiting for, boy?' and I say, 'My uncle.' He says, 'What's your uncle's name?' and I made up some name, Johnny somethin' or other. Well, that cop put his hand under my chin, lifted my head up, and said real calm-like, 'You ran away from home, didn't you, boy?'"

"Wow," I said, shaking my head in mock disbelief.

"Let me tell you, I broke down and sobbed my eyes out. They called my mom and she said she didn't have a son by that name. You see, I'd given him my full name and nobody called me by that name. When I heard that, I just about lost it, thinking that my mom had abandoned me."

"What happened?"

"When she woke up enough to realize I was gone, she called back and they had to come pick me up. That wasn't the only time, either. When I was fifteen, I couldn't take my dad's abuse anymore, so I left home and hitchhiked all the way from Maryland to Denver. They didn't catch up to me until about three months later."

He paused for a moment in thought.

"The day after my parents caught me the first time, when I was four or five, we took a road trip down to Florida. The whole way there, my dad told me the police were coming to get me and that they would put me in prison for life for running away like I did. Every time I saw a police car, I was literally petrified. And you know what I realize now?"

"What?"

"When no police caught me on our way to Florida, my little four-year-old mind learned that if you run long enough and far enough, you can outrun everyone and everything."

"That's interesting," I said, nodding my head slightly. This really was pretty interesting, even to my know-it-all mind.

There was a long pregnant pause. Lloyd looked at his desk in deep contemplation for several seconds and then snapped out of it, blinking his eyes.

"That's right," he said, clapping his hands together. "But, such is life, my friend. I'm absolutely happy with my life. You have to roll with what life gives you. If you try to make the right choices, you'll be fine. You have a bright future ahead of you, Kevin. Don't waste it."

"Yes, sir. I'm trying not to."

"Okay, enough of my prattling," he said with a chuckle. Drop that thing right here and I'll take a look at it. I'll get it back to you today. Thanks, Kevin."

"No problem, Lloyd. Have a good one," I said, making my exit.

On the way back to my desk, I saw Amber walking toward me in the same row of desks.

*Should I stop and say something, or just give her a nod? Decide quickly, you fool*, I argued with myself.

"Hi, Amber." I said, raising my finger in the air to indicate that I wanted to stop and talk.

"Oh, hey, Kev. What's up?"

*Just come out with it*, I told myself, trying to work up courage.

"Well, I was wondering if you'd like to go out with me sometime," I said with a confidence that surprised even me.

"I would love to. To be honest, I was hoping you would ask me," she replied, flipping her hair with her finger.

"Great. What are you doing this weekend?"

"Um, nothing."

"Rad. Let's go out on Saturday. Cool?"

"Yeah, sounds great. Here's my number. Do you have a pen?"

"Yeah, here."

"Here you go," she said, taking my hand and writing her phone number on my palm.

"Awesome. I definitely won't forget to call you now," I said.

"You better not!"

I returned to my desk almost floating. That was easy. There was nothing to it. She was waiting for me to ask. The rest of the day passed so quickly that I barely noticed Lloyd when he stopped by to drop the report on my desk.

"Here you go, hot shot. Have yourself a good day," he said.

"Thanks, Lloyd. I will. You have a good one, too."

When he was gone, I began looking through the stalest accounts again. I had devised a way to keep track of all the target accounts by leaving the page and line numbers for the next score on inconspicuous sticky notes scattered around my desk. I would write something innocuous such as, "118th butter A the market," or something about school like, "Remember paper on Tort Law 276 G." When I had harvested that account, I would crumple the note up and put it in my pocket to throw away someplace else. This was the first evolution in the refinement of my thievery.

# CHAPTER 4

# getting in deeper

"Yo, K man!" Donny's voice boomed on the phone.

"What it is, Donny Rocket?"

"Ah, as I look over this beautiful land I can't help but realize that I am alooone," he sang as high as he could. "Why am I able to waste my energy to notice life being so beautiful? Maybe partying will help. What are you doing tonight?"

"What was that song you were singing?"

"Dude," Donny said, disgusted at my lack of knowledge. "What? Haven't you ever listened to the Minutemen? Where you been? What're you, too busy listening to 'Flock of Seagulls' or something over there? C'mon dude."

"Oh right. Well, actually, I have a date tonight," I retorted.

"What? Since when? With who?" His shock was a little insulting.

"This girl at work," I said, nonchalantly.

"Nice, big dog. Go get 'em. Hey, you seen Paul lately? What's up with that guy? All he wants is lobster. Lobster this, lobster that. All he does is eat lobster. I'm talkin' breakfast, lunch, dinner. He is a genu-wine lobster man. That's his nickname now, 'Lobster man.' Where's he getting all this money all of a sudden, anyway? Fixing up the Trans Am, lobster for every meal, the guy's going nuts."

"Lobster man," I said, letting out a little laugh. "I'm going to start calling him that too. Hey man, gotta go. I've got to pick her up at seven."

"Alright, talk to you later biiig doggieee."

I pulled up in my gleaming, recently detailed Saab and hopped out, doing my best to exude the appropriate confidence to match the new image I was forming for myself. Amber's petite figure shone brilliantly in the reddish hue of the setting sun. She was wearing a form-fitting skirt that came down to her knees and a purple blouse with shoulder pads which gave her an aspect of seriousness. Her hair was a crazy, tousled mop of dirty blond curls that sat sideways on her head, which dwarfed her pretty, small-featured face.

Her makeup gave her away, though. It was poorly done in a pitifully cute way. Girls like Amber lack the guile for conspiracies of the body.

"Hi, Kevin!"

"Hey Amber, you look beautiful," I said, giving her a feeble hug. The protocol for dates with girls you know in a different capacity, like work, was beyond my social IQ.

"Thanks, I got this blouse yesterday at Mervyns," she purred, turning from side to side to give me the full effect.

"Here," I said, motioning to the passenger side door as if she needed help locating it. "Let me get that for you." I opened the door for her and closed it behind her gently.

"I hope you like sushi."

"Are you kidding? I looove sushi."

"Choice! Have you ever been to Hiro?"

"Never, but I've heard of it. My friend Liz told me it was amazing."

"It is. If you love sushi, it's the place to go."

The conversation in the car ride to Hiro was sporadic, mostly focusing on gossip and the goings on from work, a subject we were both relieved to have in common.

I had been on dates in the past and knew all too well the pain of uncomfortable silence. The last worthy thing is said about a subject and having nothing to bring up next feels like going off a cliff into the abyss. The silence is like a living thing; a great humidity growing bigger and more pregnant with every passing second, scoffing at your inability to come up with something pertinent to say. As the time passes, so does the necessity to say something important, or funny, or relevant. Both parties recognize this and their minds race to find something to penetrate the awful silence.

This void is where men get in trouble. Most women have a fantastic intuition and seem to always know the appropriate thing to say next. A man, however, in his desperation, will say something ridiculous, rude, or just plain dumb to make the woman prefer the silence.

My date with Amber never recessed into uneasy silence, but the conversation didn't thrill either. We sat, Indian-style around the squat Japanese table, and after a couple drinks we were both relaxed. Even though I was giving her my best material, most of my jokes fell flat. I had to explain a few of them, which is never good. She even forced herself to give me a few laughs out of courtesy. The date was pleasant enough, but as the night ended, I think we both knew things would not progress, so with a simple goodnight, we parted and I sped off in the Saab.

The thievery continued to snowball, and our confidence grew a little more each time that Paul and I got away with it. A haze came over both of our minds that told us it would never end. We made deposits and withdrawals with such regularity that it started to lose the feeling of illegality. Yes, we were sneaking around and covering our tracks, but doing it over and over again without a hitch made us loose and relaxed. It was like an extension of my 9-5 job: file papers, get coffee, steal money, balance accounts, and write checks for myself. Rinse and repeat.

Our lifestyles became ridiculous as the cash flow fed our invincible egos. We were spending all the money by going to the best clubs, buying the most expensive clothes, and upgrading our cars. Paul's new passion, besides lobster, was his Trans Am. We made fun of him by calling him "Trans-American" in our best Spanish accents and saying, "You love Trans-Americans," to which he would reply, "You know." He had just installed an all-electronic dashboard in his car, so his speedometer, RPMs, and fuel levels were displayed in oversized red digits. We drove around at night staring like dopes at the dashboard and testifying to each other about the insane degree of "rad-ness" happening before our very eyes.

There was so much money coming in, I didn't even know what to do with it all. Paul literally ate lobster tail every day and when I saw him, I would ask, "Hey lobster man, what're you doing? You have any lobster last night, buddy?"

"Oh yeah, I had a bunch last night."

"Was it good?"

"Yeah it was great. It was incredible. I bought a $100 lobster tail. The thing was so succulent."

"Wow, great," I would say.

We both appreciated and nurtured each other's stupid vices. I had "Lobster Man" bibs and T-shirts made and presented them to Paul, who wore them with pride. Neither of us ever said to the other, "Hey look, do you think you're spending too much over here?" On the contrary, we encouraged each other to find another indulgence.

"Invest in something frivolous!"

"Drain all this money as fast as you can!"

"Live it up while you can, cuz you sure as heck can't take it with you!"

We both became obsessed with health food and natural supplements, too. We were the first in line to purchase every new advancement in natural health. We spent hundreds on vitamins, minerals, Açai juice, fish oils, amino acids, teas, and every herb imaginable. We were taking supplements for things we didn't even have. "Hmm, Black Cohosh is good for menopause? Throw it in the basket!"

I bought handfuls of those B-Complex tubes at $10 a pop that you would stick up your nose and snort for a quick, natural energy boost. Of course, the effects of these overpriced elixirs were negligible, but I see now that these were desperate attempts to make myself an invincible, all-powerful superman.

The idea of the superman or the "overman" is one of the central concepts of Friedrich Nietzsche. In his book *Thus Spoke Zarathustra*, the protagonist praises the superman for rising above the normal man, who is filled with his "shameful humanity." He famously declared that "God is dead" and we should look within ourselves to overcome our beastly nature and create new values in God's absence. The superman is the one who sees past the limiting conventions of human behavior. He acts outside of it as a warrior, inventor, artist, or extraordinary individual, to push mankind and transcend the limits of traditional morality, class, creed, and nationality.

Again, this was not a conscious motivation on my part at the time, but all of this was influenced my judgment. I believed I could be the overman by drawing on my own strength and understanding. I could operate outside these paltry societal and religious edicts. I was not one of the herd. I knew better.

My dream of becoming an FBI agent remained first and foremost in my mind. I had an illusion that by doing the right thing and giving these refunds back to their rightful owners, Navarro would recognize this selfless act and reward my ingenuity by fast-tracking me to the top. I had tried everything to get noticed, but so far my efforts were futile. *How can I impress a guy like this?* I wondered.

Navarro was an old-fashioned lawman whose methods were sometimes controversial, but his results were not. This was a guy who ordered the Broward County Sheriff's Office (BSO) to start manufacturing crack cocaine to be used in sting operations. He personally, gun in hand, led drug raids, fugitive captures, and bust-ups of gay nightclubs.

While he was sheriff, the BSO's staff doubled to 3,000 employees and the budget went from $72 million to over $200 million. He was a guy who saw politicians and bureaucracy as his main roadblock to fighting crime and any method that got results was never off the table. Because of this, he was investigated by the feds and every internal investigation team available, but was never convicted of any wrong doing.

Navarro came from humble beginnings. He left Cuba as a young college student in 1950, and came to the United States to live with his sister. He was drafted into the Army and fought in the Korean War. In 1958, he moved to Florida and joined the Miami police force as a beat patrolman.

After a few years he was selected as a Miami-based federal narcotics agent, a job that involved him in undercover operations in New York, France, Lebanon, and Latin America.

He says he was truly born one day in 1964 when a heroin dealer, who discovered he was an undercover cop, put a .25-caliber pistol in his stomach and pulled the trigger. The cartridge ended up being a dud. Navarro tackled the dealer, wrestled the gun from him, and brought him in. A year later, he was shot in the leg during a drug raid in the Bronx.

He rose up the ranks and eventually headed up the county's organized crime division until elected sheriff in 1984. He reveled in publicity. If there was a spotlight near him, he was sure to fill it. He was the first sheriff to allow cameras from the TV show *Cops* to film his officers. He famously arrested the rap group 2 Live Crew in a case that went all the way to the Supreme Court.

So, this was my dilemma. How do I impress a guy who likes to bend the rules, but does so in service to a strict moral code?

This was not a guy who was easily impressed, especially by a young punk pencil-pusher like me.

After a couple months I struck upon an idea. We would take the money we were skimming off the accounts and invest it. Paul and I were two smart guys. We could take the money, invest it, have more than enough for ourselves, and not only replace the money we stole, but make money for the Sheriff's coffers at the same time.

If Navarro asked where the money came from, I would tell him everything except for the part about lining my pockets. He would be so pleased with my brilliant inventiveness that he would surely promote me. I would soon be at the right hand of one of the most powerful and visible law enforcement officers in the country. From this distinguished perch, a position at the FBI could not be far off.

I ran the idea by Paul and he was game for it. We were two young guys, so the idea of making a name for ourselves by researching and investing large sums of money seemed very mature, and in fitting with our image as little "Gordon Gekkos."

Paul dove headfirst into researching good stocks. We started by buying shares in IBM and Burdines, and opened an account with the ill-gotten gains at Charles Schwab using fake social security numbers for the names Raul Cinfuentes and Ira Cohen. We got a little tip that American Motors Corporation was about to be bought out by Chrysler, so we scrambled and bought as many shares as we could at $5 a share on margin. Essentially, we borrowed money using stolen money in a gamble to increase our pilfered funds. I wouldn't recommend it.

When the buyout happened, the stock shot up and we made close to $50,000 almost overnight. If our egos were not inflated enough, this gave them an extra boost and made us feel invincible. I was King Midas; everything I touched turned to gold. Navarro would be more than pleased. With the money we made, we set about returning some of the stolen money, putting it back into the suspense account. The new goal was to use the stolen money to invest, line our pockets, and then return the principal with no one the wiser.

One of my father's favorite pastimes was going to the track to bet on the horses and greyhounds. Sometimes he would bring me along for a little father-son bonding time. On one of these occasions, I met a jockey named Monica.

Monica was one of the top jockeys in Canada and had come down to South Florida to be a "bug rider," an apprentice jockey who is entitled to carry less weight. When I met her, she was riding horses at the Hollywood Gulfstream Racetrack for a living. She was a tiny girl, but her personality more than made up for her lack of size. Her voice had a strength behind it that made people listen to what she had to say, and she possessed a scathing wit which could cut anyone down in a matter of a sentence or two. Her wild, disheveled shock of brownish blonde hair and overly-tanned body hid her Canadian heritage and gave her the look of a Miami native.

She was what you would call a "fashionista." Her existence was centered around wearing the right clothes, going to the right restaurants, driving the right car, and being with the right man. She asked me out. Actually, she didn't ask. It was more of a demand. The second time we met at the track, she came up to me and shouted in my ear above the din of the racing horses, the uptight gamblers, and screaming vendors.

"Are you going to take me out or what?" she asked.

"Are you asking me out?"

"No, but I know you want to ask me out, so I'm saving you the trouble and embarrassment."

"How do you know I want to ask you out? I don't even know you."

"You never will if you don't ask me out. And I wouldn't want to deprive you of the incredible joy of knowing me. Maybe you don't know it yet, but I'm a real catch."

"How's that?"

"Well, as you can already see, I'm shy and demure. I don't ask for anything. Um, and, let's see, I'm a cheap date."

"You forgot about incredibly modest."

"Oh yeah, incredibly modest."

"Well, that's quite a resume."

"WHAT? I CAN'T HEAR YOU."

"I SAID, 'THAT'S QUITE A RESUME!'" I shouted, drawing a few glances from passersby as the cacophony of the race faded.

"I know. Sooooo, you have anything you want to say to me?" she said, turning her feet inwards toward each other and kicking the ground like a little kid. She looked up at me expectantly.

"Okay," I replied slowly. This was uncharted territory for me. "How's dinner sound? You free on Friday?"

"Dinner sounds good. Pick me up at 8:00, okay? I live in an apartment at the Hollywood Towers. I'll wait for you outside. You better not be late," she said with a smile.

"Don't worry, I'll be there."

When I pulled up to the rather dilapidated Hollywood Towers at 8:10 for our date, Monica was standing out front with her arms crossed.

"You're late, Mr. Cross."

"Ten minutes. C'mon."

"I'll let it slide this time, but I can't say if the universe will forgive you. It's bad karma. You know that, right? Nice car, by the way."

"Thanks. I don't know about karma. I know about traffic."

"You don't believe in karma? Listen, the universe has a balance," she said, cocking her head to eye me like a teacher to a student. "If you do something bad, it will come back to you, right? If you do something good, something good will happen to you. It's all cause and effect, man."

"Okay, I guess I can see that. But it seems too simple. What if you do something good for one person but it affects someone else in a bad way? Who decides what outweighs what? Is doing something for a child or someone helpless better than helping some guy on Wall Street? Is there some big balance sheet in the universe keeping tabs of every little strike against you? What if …"

"Slow down, slow down. It's a force that lives in everything or something. I don't know exactly, I just know it works. Anyway, this is too heavy a subject, dude. We just met each other. Tell me about yourself."

"Well, my name is Kevin and I'm an alcoholic."

"Hi, Kevin!" she said, giving me the requisite clap of the hands.

"No really, I work at the Sheriff's Office."

"Get out of here! Really? I never would have guessed. Should I be scared or something?"

"Don't worry, I only arrest people I don't like," I said, giving her a raised eyebrow.

"Hmm. I better watch myself then."

"Don't forget it. Actually, I'm just an accountant in the Civil Division."

"Ha! Well, can't do much harm from there can you?" she said, punching me playfully on the arm.

"Yeah, guess not."

I took Monica to see *Gorillas in the Mist* at the Florida Twin Cinema at the Hollywood Mall. During the movie my nerves began to get the best of me.

*What am I doing with a twenty-seven year-old woman?* I asked myself. How could I possibly impress her? She had traveled the world. She was cultivated and refined, well-read and educated. I was a nineteen-year-old kid still living at my parents' house with no idea where the path I was embarking on would lead me. It was exhilarating, yet overwhelming.

These thoughts spun furiously around my head, making me dizzy and rendering me physically ill. Several times during the movie, I thought I would vomit right in the aisle or on Monica's Italian leather shoes. After the movie, she had to walk me to the car, drive me home, and drop me off at my parents' house. I laboriously dragged myself out of the car, thoroughly ashamed, and unceremoniously muttered something unintelligible as a farewell. She watched as my hunched frame shuffled to the door and disappeared inside.

The next day, she miraculously appeared at the door, full of concern about my condition. My mother ushered her in to see me and I kept telling her, "I'm fine, it must have just been a little twenty-four-hour bug. Don't worry." The truth was, though, that I had made a miraculous recovery not ten minutes after she left the night before. This was no bug. It was the manifestation of the fear of what I was becoming. My body was reacting the way my mind should have to this new lifestyle of lies, facades, and deception.

When I was sixteen, I started drinking and dabbling in drugs during college with Tommy, Jason, Charlie, and other guys from the neighborhood and Christian school. It was mostly marijuana, and usually just an occasional thing every other weekend, or when one of the guys got his hands on something. We were too young and poor to afford much, so our tastes were satiated with cheap booze and an occasional joint.

Once, in our idiocy, we even tried to make our own dope from banana skins taken from the banana tree in my backyard. We followed a recipe that had been passed around by hippie high school kids since the sixties, which instructed us to scrape off the inside of a banana peel and boil it for several hours until it became a paste. We cooked the paste in the oven until it was a powder and then smoked it. The recipe turned out to be an urban legend, and we quickly learned that bananas are for eating and nothing else.

In those days, I foolishly viewed drugs as a necessary step of coming of age. Almost all the kids I knew used them in some form or another. For that matter, so did most of the adults. In those days in Miami, drugs had no clear target when it came to class, creed, income level, or color. Lawyers, Wall Street executives, and housewives were all in on it.

I had dabbled in some heavier drugs as well, but always stayed on the periphery and never descended into habitual use. Now, with a new influx of money, everything became easier to obtain and money was no longer an obstacle to procuring what we wanted, when we wanted it. The day after our first date, Monica brought me back to her closet-sized apartment, and within its cramped confines, I experienced the pleasures of this world.

She introduced me to a more sophisticated and acceptable way of debauchery in the form of fine liqueurs like Sambuca and Frangelico. Sambuca was a liqueur made from licorice that would burn your throat even when it's ice cold, and Frangelico was a sickeningly sweet liqueur made from hazelnut that came in a bottle shaped like a friar. Together we also acquired a taste for Scotch and experimented with all manner of frozen concoctions which regularly rendered me drunk or unconscious. Monica hated this, but for me, the only reason to drink was to get drunk.

Her apartment became a sanctuary for me. I would go there almost every day after work and usually stay for the night. We would sit on the floor together for hours sipping Frangelica and listening to Simply Red, Joy Division, The Smiths, and cheesy DJs. I fell in love with her to the sounds of "Holding Back the Years": "Holding back the years, Chance for me to escape from all I've known, Holding back the tears, Cause nothing here has grown."

My eyes were opening upon a brave new world, and as they adjusted to the brilliant light, I saw things I had never witnessed before. I had entered a world that resembled the famous painting by Hieronymus Bosch, *The Garden of Earthly Delights*—a scene of extraordinary beauty, but hidden under the surface lurked something unspeakably horrible. I could never put my finger on what it was, but something monstrous was moving just out of sight on my periphery, and it made me extremely uneasy.

As our relationship progressed, I began impressing her the only way I knew how—with my newfound money. With a large chunk of funny money, I bought her a Movado Museum watch and myself the Movado Esquire timepiece. We got matching Gucci 18k gold chains because that was important. She bought me a gaudy purple $100 tie, which was all the rage at the time, with a giant red and gold dragon on it. The only problem was I really couldn't draw any attention to it at work where I wore it most often.

She already had an impressive collection of jewelry, but I replaced it all with newer, hipper earrings, bracelets, necklaces, and rings. I bought her all the dresses and shoes that she loved. The more expensive or exclusive, the better.

I once took her to Lillie Rubin, an elite and ultra expensive boutique. When they started treating me like a kid, I pulled out a roll of cash, shot the manager an angry look, and said, "I am Ramone Simone. You get this dame anything she wants. Understood?"

They immediately jumped into action, ushering us back to an exclusive viewing area, complete with leather sofas and a private changing room, while serving us single malt Scotch. I drank several and got a sophisticated high that resulted in a couple thousand dollar spending spree.

Ramone Simone had now shed the leather jacket and jeans in favor of highly tailored suits. He was now a Miami-Vice-inspired, abusive, stylish high-roller with an endless bank account and a chip on his shoulder.

One day during the summer, I decided she couldn't live in her shack of an apartment anymore. I picked her up and took her to a chic apartment complex in the Young Circle area. When we walked into the rental office together, the manager eyed us suspiciously.

"Are you interested in an apartment?" he said, distractedly.

"Yeah, I'm looking for one for my girl. How much is it?" I said, fingering a giant wad of cash in my pocket.

"Kevin, you don't have to ..." Monica interjected sheepishly.

"Well, we have one bedrooms that start at $900 per month, and we have ..."

"How much if I pay you six months up front?" I said, whipping the rolled-up bills out of my pocket.

"Well," the manager stammered, "six months would be ... let me think ... we could do six months for ... $5,000."

I began peeling $100 bills out of the bundle and slapping them down on the table, counting ten at a time and making five neat piles across the manager's desk. The feeling was exhilarating. The manager, who had seen me as just a boy when I walked in, was now in complete reverence of my power. Monica just sat there, stunned and giddy.

"Who are you? What do you do?" the manager asked, respectfully now.

"My name's Ramone Simone. It's a pleasure to meet you. I'm an investor," I said arrogantly.

"My name is Francis Del'Abate. Friends call me Frank. I own the Ramona Apartments down the road," he said, handing us both a business card. "Anything you need, you call me, got it?"

After we signed the contract, I went and told my mother that I was moving out to live with Monica. She sat in her hospital clothes in her favorite Victorian chair and cried about my decision.

I told her not to worry; I would be back to visit. I assured her I wasn't doing anything wrong and walked out the door, closing it behind me to the muffled sound of her sobs.

The slippery slope just got a little slicker.

Once a year, by state law, the Civil Division of the Sheriff's Office would undergo a public certified audit by an independent accounting firm, an occurrence which set the entire office buzzing. That year, I was assigned to give the auditor anything he needed and act as his assistant during the two-month-long process. I wasn't really worried. Even if they thoroughly investigated, there was nothing to find. The hard drives that contained the suspense accounts had been wiped clean of any accounts that could possibly raise suspicion.

The auditor loved having a protégé, so he allowed me to pal around with him as he did his job, extolling the virtues of his line of work. Several times he told me, "Someday, if you play your cards right, you could be an auditor, too. It's a great field. You gotta be smart and you gotta keep your eyes open."

He took me under his wing, and during the two months he was in and out of the office, he taught me many things to look for when you suspect that the books might be cooked; tips for getting past common hiding techniques and a few little tricks for catching embezzlers.

*I'll make a mental note of that, thank you*, I thought.

He treated me to lunch one day and we drove over to a ribs place in his brand new 1989 Ford Escort.

"Nice car," I said.

"Yeah, it's a really nice car," he bragged, running his hand along the steering wheel affectionately. "You'll be able to get one of these someday."

I just smiled and nodded.

One day during the audit, Melvin, the front desk officer, stopped me with a grave look on his face as I was arriving for work.

"Kevin, wait a second. I've got to talk to you about something."

*Oh, no*, I thought, *this can't be good*. Visions of the worst-case scenario flashed in my head. This was it. I tried to sneak a glance at my desk to see if it was surrounded by officers and bosses. I imagined Navarro himself standing at my desk, and noticing me, raising his arm in slow motion to point me out to the other officers.

I could see his mouth forming the words, "That's the guy right there."

*It can't go down like this*, I thought. *Not in front of everyone at work*. I could just hear the interviews with the press:

"He sat across from me for a year," Phyllis would say, dabbing her eyes emotionally. "He was the sweetest boy. You would never guess he had it in him to do something like this. Such a shame."

Melvin noticed my distracted look.

"Kevin, you okay, my man?"

"Yeah, yeah, I'm good. Just a little tired."

"Anyway, I wanted to ask you. My Vo-Tech school is looking for someone to teach their accounting class one night a week. I immediately thought about you and thought maybe you'd be interested."

"What? Really? Well, I guess so. Honestly, I'm not sure if I'm qualified," I stammered in shock and relief.

"Well, just think about it. The woman you need to contact is Josie. Give her a call if you think you can do it," Melvin said, handing me a business card.

"Thanks for thinking of me, Melvin, I will give her a call. Have a good one."

I was shocked by how rattled it made me. My heart pounded for about a half an hour. Maybe I wasn't as at ease with this and as secure as I had thought.

That was the first moment I felt the ground moving beneath me, and a creeping dread lodged itself at the base of my spine that never went away. It began as a little tingle, but I knew it would keep growing every day until I was consumed by it.

Maybe Lady Fortuna's wheel was starting to turn me upside down. Maybe I was wrong. Maybe I wasn't the overman. Perhaps

Monica was right and it was karma coming back to me. I had escaped a bullet this time, but the gnawing fear of getting caught was eating away in my gut.

CHAPTER 5

# money is no object

November 19, 1986. My twentieth birthday.

I picked up Tommy and Jason, who were for some reason without Charlie Moreno that night, to go to City Limits, an upscale club in Fort Lauderdale. Monica didn't come either. We had been fighting about my drinking and she was punishing me by not celebrating my birthday. She complained that I was drinking too much. I defended myself, saying that I wasn't drinking enough. We just couldn't find any middle ground on the issue, so I was staying at my parents' house until everything blew over.

We rarely went to City Limits because my fake ID, which was actually the Sheriff's Office badge with my brother Kirk's birth date haphazardly glued onto it, didn't work in the nicer places. But this was the first birthday I had had some expendable cash, so I was going to make it a memorable one. I went with $1,000 cash in my pocket with the intention of coming back with nothing. The Saab 900S, my eternal source of pleasure, was souped up with every possible upgrade known to mankind.

We pulled up to the valet, the White Demon purring like a kitten, and eased out like we had seen a thousand times on *Miami Vice*. I threw the keys at the valet.

*Poor schmuck loser has to wear that red vest and do the "ten-hut" to every jerk that comes in here*, I thought. Jerks like me.

I turned to Tommy and Jason.

"Watch this. Hey valet! Wait a second."

"Yes, sir?"

"I've got a proposition for ya. I'll give you a $50 tip if you can park the car and be back here in less than two minutes."

"Really? But the garage is a quarter mile away."

"I don't care. That's not my problem. Hussle. Do what you gotta do. And don't scratch my baby, okay?"

"Yes, sir," he groaned.

"Ready?" I said, checking my Movado. "And go."

As the valet scrambled to get into the car and start it, we laughed, doing impressions of his humiliated face and cracking ourselves up.

Two minutes and thirty-five seconds later, the frazzled valet returned, running at full speed and sucking wind. He was drenched in sweat.

"Did I make it?" he puffed.

"Sorry, kid. Maybe next time," I said, turning around and heading into the club with Tommy and Jason.

We strode right up to the bar brimming with confidence.

"I'll have a Tom Collins, and vodka and cranberry juice for my two friends here. Oh, and get this beautiful lady a martini," I said, motioning to a woman sitting alone at the bar. "And listen, if you do it in less than thirty seconds, there's a hundy in my pocket for you."

The bartender was not fazed like the valet had been. He whipped up the drinks in record time and I proudly slapped a hundred dollar bill down on the wet bar.

"I am a man of my word. Thank you, sir."

The bartender said nothing, but I saw everyone within eyeshot take notice of me. I fed off the power.

The night continued in this fashion. I was buying everyone drinks; my friends, women I didn't know, the women's boyfriends, even the bartender. After a few rounds, everyone was wasted and I became the center of attention for everyone at the bar. I was everybody's pal for one night. I was finally the big shot I had always dreamed of being.

Eventually, near closing time, Tommy and Jason and I were sitting in a booth together.

"So, Kevin. What's the story, man? We're starving students, dude. Where are you getting all this dough?" Tommy asked above the dance music.

"Yeah, we know you're poor. Your family is poor. What's up?" Jason chimed in.

"I ain't doing nothin' guys, just a little investing. I'm buyin' stocks and whatnot," I slurred.

"Well, you gonna cut us in or what? You gonna tell us how to invest? I mean, we're dyin' here, you know?" Tommy prodded.

"Well, well ... really I don't know what I'm doing. Just ... luck ..." I managed to spit out. "Wait, whawetalkin ... boutagain? I forgot ..." Even in my drunken state, I told myself not to say anything.

"Tell us about the money you're throwing around. What are you doing?"

*How were these guys so sober*, I wondered.

"Oh, yeah, the money. I really don't ... I'm not ... this thing here, well. It's just luck, ya know?"

"Luck, schmuck! C'mon, level with us. It's Tommy and Jason here. We've known you since elementary school," Jason said.

"Yeah, throwin' $100 bills around like they's toilet paper ain't no luck I ever seen, you Jason?" Tommy said with a laugh.

"Not me, I never seen it," Jason replied.

The waitress came around with our drink order; three shots of Jägermeister, which we promptly downed.

"Here's to Kevin!"

"Here's to Kevin, the man with the master plan."

I have to admit, it felt good to have my ego stroked a little. I was full of pride. These were guys that I looked up to my whole life for their nice houses and fancy cars and beautiful lives, when I was poor and ugly. Finally, I had something they wanted. I was impressive to them.

"So, c'mon man, you gonna come clean with us, pal? What's the secret?" Tommy wouldn't let up.

"Okay, listen. I'm 'onna telya, but this is … top secret, right?" I whispered, hovering my finger in front of my lips. "Ya know my job workin' for the Sheriff?"

"Yeah, yeah, yeah."

"Well, listen to this …" I was sobering up as I began to spill my guts. "Paul and I found a way to access a li'l money that nobody's using. It's an account for, like, deposits to the Sheriff for services. They owe money to a lot, a lotta people. People who're dead or lef' town, so that money is just sittin' there. It's never, ever gonna be used …"

"I *knew* Paul was doing something," Tommy said, like he had solved a puzzle. "I talked to him and he wouldn't tell me anything. Kev, this is radical, man. Tell us everything," he urged, leaning in closer.

And I did. I explained every detail of the scheme and how Paul was helping me deposit the checks. It felt liberating to tell someone who could admire the beauty of the thing. They wanted me to cut them in, but I told them there wasn't enough to go around.

"I'll … I'll take you out to dinner or something. I'll buy you a drink," I faltered.

"Take us out to dinner?" Tommy said, exchanging an offended look with his brother. "We know you, what, eleven years, and you say 'I'll take you out to dinner'? Are you kidding me?"

"Yeah, man," echoed Jason indignantly.

"Look, guys. There's only so much money. I can't take any more than what I already get and I have to split that with Paul, so, you know," I mumbled, staring down at the pool of beer that had formed on the table.

The table fell silent. Tommy and Jason just sat there looking perturbed, while I just stared vacantly at the people dancing a few feet away. I couldn't believe this reaction. I had hurt my good friends because I wouldn't cut them in on my embezzlement scheme? I worried for a second that I had made a grave mistake by letting the cat out of the bag, but I knew they wouldn't get me in trouble. These were good friends. I had known them forever. This was just the alcohol talking.

After a few more rounds, we left as the club happily closed the doors behind us. We went outside to the valet and got the car. Luckily, it was a different valet than the earlier one, so I was spared the embarrassment. I hopped into the driver's seat, Jason stumbled into the front passenger seat, and Tommy slid into the back.

The exit from City Limits was a Y intersection. One way went west on Miami Avenue and the other went east. I veered to the left to go east because it intersected with US1, one of the busiest roads in the area and the one I would take home. At the end of the service road was another Y. One way led to a dead end and the other was Miami Avenue.

In my drunkenness, I steered the car down what I thought was a dead end, only it wasn't really a dead end. It dumped me out on to US1. *This is perfect*, I thought. *This is right where I am supposed to be. I never knew I could go this way.*

I vaguely saw headlights coming at me and remember hearing the blaring of car horns, but they seemed otherworldly, just blurs off in the distance. Suddenly, I realized that several cars were heading right at us and that I was, in fact, driving northbound on a southbound road.

I jerked the wheel to the right with as much force as I could muster. I was driving at least 45-50 miles per hour, and the force of the turn threw a seatbelt-less Tommy across the backseat into the window. As the car careened into the massive median, I felt a huge jolt and the earsplitting shriek of metal scraping concrete as the wheels bowed and broke completely off; jumping and whizzing down the highway, forcing several cars to swerve wildly to avoid them.

We skidded violently across the grassy patch in the median and then down to the other side of the road. The car was entirely out of my control as we tore across two lanes of southbound traffic. All I could perceive through my haze was a fog of bright lights and the squeal of tires.

I don't know how, but over the deafening clamor, I uttered a lightning fast, almost subconscious, wordless prayer to the God of my childhood. It was a desperate, soulful plea, something like, "Please don't let anything happen to me 'cause I don't deserve to die like this."

The car continued to skid for another thirty feet, miraculously dodging oncoming traffic, and lurching into a parking lot at an old, abandoned office building. It was over as soon as it began, and everything became eerily quiet.

After several stunned seconds, the shock wore off and I checked myself for injuries. Miraculously, I hadn't even received a scratch. Tommy and Jason had also escaped injury and didn't seem to realize how close we had come to being killed. They both shot me confused looks as if to say, "What are we doing in a parking space? Let's go already."

Oddly, the first thing I thought about wasn't that I was safe, or that I hadn't injured or killed anyone. Instead, I was upset about the expense I would have to incur to repair my most prized possession in this world, the Saab. I climbed out of the car and saw the faint yellow lines where a parking space used to be. We had stopped dead center inside the space, and in front of a small, rusted metal sign that ironically read "Reserved."

As I looked at the crumpled metal, I felt ruined. Where there were once wheels, all that remained were mangled metal stumps that were still smoking. The smell of red hot metal and melting rubber assaulted my nostrils as I beheld my fallen god.

This car held the keys to my significance and satisfaction. I had poured everything I was into it, and so my self-image was tied in with it. Every upgrade, every glamorous addition was another twisted appendage of my ego. Its tendrils had grown through me until they enveloped my very soul.

At a time when my bank account was swelling, I suffered from the ultimate poverty of the soul. All I could think about were the financial implications of the crash. I had just narrowly escaped my death, the death of the occupants of my car, and the death of innocents, yet my mind only focused on fixing the car that represented my god. It wasn't my only god, I had many, but this god offered me a satisfaction and pleasure that I could never find in any hokey religion.

My mangled car was unmovable. I would have to call the next day to get it towed. I took a cab ride to my parents house since, even in my punch-drunk state, I knew going home to Monica was a bad idea. I threw a $20 tip at the driver and staggered to the door. I don't even know what happened to Tommy and Jason. Thankfully, everyone was asleep as I crept back into the house. The crash sobered me up, so all my faculties for sneaking were at full power.

I delicately eased the door open, and slowly shut it behind me, waiting for the lock to pop faintly into place. The house was dead quiet. It was an old house with wood floors, but from my years of tiptoeing through the house, I had a perfect mental picture of the rooms and could navigate them in silence, avoiding every creaky board. I got to my room, closed the door, and fell on my bed.

I tried to shut my eyes tightly and forget the night, but when I did, the room started spinning out of control, free-falling into nothing. The nauseous sensation was all too familiar, and I already knew what I had to do. Foregoing any attempt at stealth, I threw open the door and rushed to the bathroom. I almost made it in time.

The contents of my stomach, which were mostly sickeningly sweet liquors and beer, came violently gushing out, far surpassing the voracity with which I had consumed them. When I had finished, my exhausted body just slumped down. I braced myself against the edge of the bathtub and through my blurred vision, I remember staring at the strange contour of the toilet and the huge purple shower curtain, studying their shapes and thinking about where I had gone wrong.

Was this a karmic, cosmic punishment for my misdeeds? Was it dumb luck, or just sheer, random coincidence? Was it the jealous God of my youth punishing me for having idols and other gods? I looked up at a little frame hanging across from the toilet, which had a little cross stitch my mom had done. It read, "As for me and my house, we will serve the Lord."

I grew up in a Christian household, so I had heard and read about deathbed repentance, clichéd jailhouse conversions, or rebirths after a major life catastrophe, and I always thought of those people as suckers. While everyone else was crying in church about these stories of redemption, I was secretly incredulous inside. They were only using God as a big fat emotional crutch to get them out of a jam. The minute they were back on their feet, they'd go back to their other gods.

I swore I would never let this happen to me. I'd gotten through life so far without God's help, so I was sure I could handle this on my own. No toilet-side conversions for me. I was stronger than that.

My ruminating was interrupted by another fit of nausea, only this time there was nothing to throw up. I heaved uncontrollably, gasping desperately for air in between thrusts, only getting just enough before I was forced to expel it again. This continued for several interminable minutes, which I thought could seriously be my last.

My obituary would read: "Kevin Cross, beloved son, law school student, found dead on bathroom floor clutching a purple shower curtain. Highly intelligent, articulate, and witty, Kevin could have risen to great heights if he had not stolen thousands from the Sheriff, gotten drunk, spilled the beans to two Italian fellas, and crashed his car going the wrong way on a one-way street. He is survived by his white Saab 900S with 22-inch rims and all-leather interior. He will be missed."

Finally the fit subsided and I got my breath again. The night continued on like this, lying on the bathroom floor, alternately vomiting and philosophizing, with the ensuing outcome of both the same.

≈

I awoke with a jolt to hear someone shaking the bathroom doorknob.

"Kevin? Is that you in there? What are you doing here?" I heard the muffled voice of my mother on the other side of the door.

"Yeah, it's me, Ma. Just a second, okay?"

"You okay in there?"

"Yeah, just fine. I'll be right out. Just give me a second," I moaned, trying to get out of the awkward position I had gotten myself into. My arms were splayed out in both directions on the edge of the bathtub, head angled back at ninety degrees, and legs propped up on the toilet. Everything hurt as I struggled to get on my feet.

I did a quick cleanup, washed my hands, examined my face in the mirror, and opened the door to face my mother.

"Honey, I'm heading to work. You sleep okay? When did you get here? I didn't know you were coming. I didn't hear you come in last night," she said, fixing my disheveled hair with a loving hand.

"Sure, I slept just fine."

"Well," she said, giving me a motherly checkup with her eyes, "I've got eggs and bacon on the table. Eat some before you take off, okay?"

"Will do, Ma. Thanks," I said, giving her a kiss on the forehead.

We paused for a long second, regarding each other in the hallway outside the bathroom before she went in and closed the door.

The smell of eggs and bacon was too much for my beleaguered stomach to handle. I quickly grabbed the Yellow Pages and ducked into my old room. I laid the Yellow Pages on the bed next to the phone and flipped through to "tires." Finding a place about a mile from the wreckage, I picked up the phone and called.

"Goodyear," the man answered. "How can I help you?"

"Yeah, you guys do towing? I need you to pick up my car."

"Yep, we'll pick it up. What's the problem?"

"Well, I need tires. Actually, I probably need wheels too. Do you guys do wheels? It's a Saab 900S."

"Yes sir, we've got wheels for you."

"Good, good. Because I want the best wheels you got. The car's white. I need white wheels. And rims. I want white rims, too. Can you guys lower it while you're fixing it?" My excitement grew at the thought of reconstructing my beloved god into something even more glorious.

"Depends. You mean low profile wheels? We can do everything, but it's gonna cost you. You're looking at … let me see … they don't make white rims for that car. We'll have to paint them which'll be $100 each rim, so you're lookin' at probably $2,500 for all the parts and then we'll see about the labor. I can't tell you that yet. We'll see when we take a look at the car."

"Fine, paint 'em. MINO. Money is no object, my man." It felt good to say that. I felt my heart and soul flood with satisfaction again. My car and my ego would rise from the ashes better than ever. I had been saved. I lived to see another day. And that day would be mine. This time it would be different. The salami slicer extraordinaire. The boy king.

I was watching TV when Goodyear called me back.

"Kevin Cross?" the voice on the other end asked.

"This is he."

"We got your car here okay, but I've got to tell you, your frame is bent something awful and the wheels are gone. What happened?"

"Oh, I hit a median."

"To bend the frame this bad, you had to have been going 50 mph or more."

"Sounds about right," I said flippantly.

"How did you not flip over? I gotta tell you, I've never seen this before.

"I dunno. It's a good car. It's a Saab."

"And you're telling me nobody was hurt?"

"Not a scratch."

"Wow, kid. You are lucky. I've never seen damage like this without a fatality, you know? You must have somebody looking out for you. Straightening the frame is at least a $1,000 job, and there's no guarantee that it'll work. We'll have to take it to a frame stretcher."

"Go ahead and straighten out the frame. I'm keeping the car, my friend. Listen, for the tires, I want Pirellis, okay? You guys sell those, don't you?"

"We'll have to order them for you. That's gonna add $300 a piece to the bill."

"No problem. How long do you think it'll take?"

"All this? Realistically? It's going to be a week or more."

"If I pay more, any chance to get it done faster?"

He let out a little laugh. "You're still looking at about a week."

"I'll come down there right now and pay you in advance if you want," I pleaded.

"Alright, we'll see what we can do."

The week dragged by slowly. I borrowed Monica's green two-seater Buick Skylark to get to work. It didn't have air conditioning, and I was embarrassed to have to roll down the window manually. I would try to hide my face at stoplights because any car but my own was not who I was.

I called Paul and told him what happened with the Saab and that I needed money. I sensed a bit of resentment for the first time in Paul's voice, but I wrote it off. Maybe he was just having a bad day. We dipped into the source yet again, and came out with more than enough to cover the car and keep my lifestyle going for another few weeks.

Goodyear finished the work on the car in just four days, and so I felt at ease again. I had dodged a bullet. Everything in my life was back on course. My car was better than ever, the woman I loved took me back, law school was going well, and our little game was still right on schedule.

The next Sunday was Mother's Day, so Paul and I decided to take our mothers to church in an act of repentance. We had not been going to church much lately, so this was a major deal for both of them. They got all dressed up in their best Sunday attire and we chauffeured them to the church we grew up in.

Paul's little sister, Katie, who absolutely idolized him and hung on his every word, came along too. She sat next to Paul and held his hand every chance she could get. Katie was blessed with the same genes Paul had. Her tiny, cherubic face was framed by long, curly brown hair that matched her big, iridescent hazel eyes. She wore a goofy smile the entire day, reveling in the time with her brother. It would have been a beautiful irony if the sermon was about the Prodigal Son, but I think it was Ephesians 4 or something.

After the service, we took everyone out for brunch at a buffet-style place. We quickly discovered a little bar serving mimosas, so we offered to fill our mother's plates, and then downed two or three mimosas at a time, telling the bartender to "hold the orange juice." At first, our behavior was just boisterous, but after a few charitable trips to the buffet line for our mothers, we started to draw attention to ourselves. Our embarrassed moms cut the brunch short and ushered us out of there. I'm not sure if they ever understood why we were acting like that because they let us drive them home.

Parents, mothers in particular, have unparalleled blinders when it comes to their children. Short of murder, mothers are miraculously able to rationalize even the most egregious behavior.

On one occasion, Paul and I got drunk and took our cars to a church's charity car wash to toss some money around. We began literally throwing the money at these high school kids raising money for their youth group. They went crazy. We tossed out $10, $20, $50 at a time, and laughed at them as they scrambled about and followed our every whim.

A long line of cars was waiting behind us, but we didn't care. We kept on this power trip, telling them, "You didn't whitewash those rims good enough yet. I want to see my face in there. Clean that window again, faster this time." Each request got more and more ridiculous.

Our fun little self-aggrandizing game ended abruptly, though, when I made a comment about a profane necklace that one of the kids was wearing. Everyone got dead silent when one of the dads got in my face and told us, "That's it! You guys are done here. Time to leave." We had dropped a few hundred on each car that day.

A relationship started to emerge between the drinking and spending. There wasn't a day that went by that I didn't indulge in the pleasures of purchasing. It was intoxicating. It was an inebriation that was not only accepted by society, it was encouraged. When I bought something new or flashed my cash, it felt just like that first drink—a sensation of warmth, followed by a brief moment of euphoria. But, like drinking, the high only lasted a little while.

I had to keep going back to the source. I was spending the money as fast as it came in, and sometimes even faster. I often felt as if I was just a go-between. The money already had a destination; I was just a courier to take it to its predestined end.

This newfound addiction found its way into my heart more than any drug or drink ever could. The rapturous power of my riches was bringing about a metamorphosis inside me, from the boy wonder to an unrecognizable monstrosity.

Soon, the booze wasn't enough. As my boredom with life increased, so did my habits. One night I sent my little friend Donny Beck, who had looked up to me with great respect, into a drug neighborhood to get us something a little stronger. I sent him because I had too much to lose, and he was expendable. I saw myself as a kid with promise. I would graduate from law school, have an accounting degree, and eventually join the FBI. He was a punk neighborhood kid who would never amount to anything.

The house Donny went to was being monitored by the police, and they decided to raid it when he was inside. They tackled him to the ground, cuffed him, and held him there for three hours before releasing him. He was a young, impressionable kid, and for all the bravado he exuded, the experience shook him to the core. When he came back shocked and shaking, I remember feeling nothing for him. Not remorse, sympathy, pity, kindness, nothing. But I was upset that he didn't get the stuff.

One day in the fall, Monica's horse fell during training and she cracked her collarbone. Jockeys live by feast or famine. If you ride and win, you make obscene amounts of money. If you ride and lose, you make nothing. If you can't ride, you make even less. She went from being a leading jockey making thousands a week to making nothing. So I found myself living with a girl I had just met, and supporting her with stolen money. In my delirious, drug and booze-fueled reality, I asked her to marry me. The lines that we had drawn in our relationship slowly became blurred and ultimately disappeared completely.

One night, we decided to go to a restaurant that had just opened on the intercoastal called Billy's Stone Crab. I had a fake ID, but that night I had no need to use it. I had made a new ID with the name Benjamin Franklin. As soon as I walked in the door, I peeled a crisp $100 bill off my wad and told the waiter, "Let me have a martini within one minute. If you make it back within a minute, you get the $100. If not, you get nothing."

All night long was a charade; a show for everyone to see how powerful I was. I made up every stupid contest I could think of just to watch the waiters degrade themselves. The people at the other tables were marveling at the amount of cash I was literally throwing out. I didn't care that I didn't even know the people who were awestruck over this costly exhibition I was putting on for their benefit.

I only remember one table in particular who was seething, furious over my disgusting display. They got up and left, very noisily discussing my prostitution of the staff. I just hope the waiters don't remember that scrawny, abusive twenty-year-old sitting across from a scantily clad, confused girl, who enjoyed watching her boyfriend demean them.

We couldn't drive home, so we left the Saab and took a taxi back. Monica fell asleep immediately, but I remember sitting up in the dark, praying to the God of my childhood. These were not prayers for forgiveness or redemption. I was praying to die.

I had everything I thought I wanted: free sex, free money, drugs, booze, endless spending money, a beautiful sports car, my own apartment, and the promise of a bright future. But I still wasn't satisfied. I pleaded with God to put me out of my misery:

"Please God, I don't know what this life is all about. What am I doing?" I prayed in my drunken state, literally writhing on the floor of my bedroom. "I don't know what I'm doing. Why am I not happy? Aren't you supposed to be a loving God? Why are you letting me suffer like this? This is your plan? If you are merciful, just end it right now. I don't care if I go to hell. Hell is better than this. Finish me off, God."

He didn't kill me like I had asked, but I had a strange feeling that maybe my prayer had been heard.

When I awoke the next morning, the prayer I uttered the night before was my first thought. I disregarded it as a shameful moment of weakness, just inebriated ramblings, something not uncommon for me in those days.

The foundation of my relationship with Monica was the proclivity we shared for basking in the warm glow of drunkenness, even when it was hidden behind fancy bottles with expensive-sounding names. To put it diplomatically, our relationship was tumultuous. We had horrendous fights, dish-shattering fights, fights that aroused the suspicions of the neighbors.

One night when Monica still lived in her small apartment, I felt unsatisfied by her, so I left her in the bed and walked to her very attractive girlfriend's apartment, an efficiency just a few doors down.

I knocked on her door, and to my pleasant surprise, she welcomed me in. I thought, *Man, this is fantastic! Two girls in one night. Every guy's fantasy.*

Soon came a pound on the door.

"Kevin, Get out! I know you're in there! Open the door right now!" Monica shrieked.

"It's not what it looks like!" I lied.

"I don't care! Come out right now!" she screeched hysterically.

When I came out, we went and got in the Saab. For two hours we sat in the car, with her screaming and throwing things at me. I was at my wit's end, making up lies and apologizing. In my uncontrollable rage, I punched the windshield of my car from the inside with my fist.

The glass made a loud crunching sound and a small fracture appeared, which upset me even more. It started small, but I knew it would grow to envelop the whole windshield. That's the thing about windshields. Once they get a little crack in them, if you don't do anything about it, it will keep spreading. You won't see it, because it comes in tiny increments that aren't noticeable. One day, you'll get in the car and the entire windshield will fall apart.

I was a scrawny 135-pound kid who was beginning to lose all control.

Looking back now, all these little episodes would have served as wake-up calls to a wiser man. They did give me pause for a moment or two, but my heart was overrun with calluses from the tiny injections of joy I had given myself with every new desire I fulfilled. My heart had become a rocky place where the things that bring true joy in this life could find no purchase. All that remained was just enough space for another injection. Over time, those shots made me forget all about remorse.

My next planned injection was a big one. Several weeks later after Monica had forgiven me, I told her, "You don't have to live in this little apartment forever. In a couple months, we will buy a house, okay?" Empty promises were my forte, but I had every intention of coming through on this one.

One morning, as I was heading out to work, I kissed my girlfriend on the forehead and said goodbye. When I opened the front door, I looked down to see a few discarded cigarette butts on the front steps.

*That's odd*, I thought. *Nobody I know smokes. What are those butts doing there? That stuff'll kill you. I would never do anything so unhealthy for my body.*

I locked the door behind me and turned toward the street to see two guys I had never seen before leaning against my Saab.

"Kevin Cross?" one of them asked.

"Yeah?"

"Get in the car."

# CHAPTER 6

# kidnapped by the mafia

One of the guys was my height, but built like a linebacker. His wavy black hair was greased back and sat on top of a scarred, pockmarked face only a mother could love. He didn't move, he just sat there staring at me, sizing me up.

The other guy was shorter than I, but had a little more beef on him, as was often the case with me. He had dark, slicked-back hair like his pal, but there was one piece of hair in the front that hung down over his face, partially blocking a massive scar running from the right corner of his mouth to the middle of his cheek.

"We wouldn't want to hurt you right here in front of your house," said the skinnier one in a thick New York accent. "We don' wanna go inside, wake your girlie up and kill her, got it? Now open the door and let us in. If you cooperate, you won't get hurt."

The thought of disobeying their orders never even entered my mind. My fumbling hands awkwardly pulled the keys out of my pocket and I walked to the driver's side door.

"Uh-uh, where do you think you're goin'? Get in the passenger side," the skinny one ordered.

I started walking to the other side of the car, my fear growing with every step.

"First open the door for my colleague here. He's gonna drive. You ain't gonna make this hard for us, are you?"

"N-no, I don't know," I stammered.

I unlocked the driver's side door and opened it for the linebacker. The seat gave out a creaking groan as he lurched into it.

"Good, good, now open the other side for me," the skinny mouthpiece barked.

He slid into the back seat, and I sat down in the front, trembling now.

I don't know what I hated more: being abducted, or having someone else drive my Saab. No one drove my Saab. It was a desecration.

As soon as we pulled out of the apartment complex, the skinny guy grabbed my head by my hair and violently turned it toward him in the backseat. I struggled to get free of his hand, but he only tightened his grip, ripping pieces of my hair out by the roots.

"LOOK AT ME!" he screamed, taking his free hand and slapping me as hard as he could from his position.

"WHAT ARE YOU DOIN'? LOOK AT ME WHEN I TALK TO YOU!"

I started to hyperventilate and gave up trying to get loose. My gasps for breath were drowned out by the skinny guy's shouts.

"WHO DO YOU THINK YOU ARE? WHO DO YOU THINK YOU ARE? HUH?"

"I don't know what you're talking about. You're hurting me," I pleaded frantically.

"I SAID, LOOK AT ME WHEN I TALK TO YOU! WHAT DO YOU THINK YOU'RE DOING?"

I tried to look at him, but all I could see was the linebacker driving the car. He just stared straight ahead, calmly smoking his cigarette, apparently oblivious to what was happening.

My eyes filled with tears as the hairs on my scalp were literally being torn from my head. I tried to close my eyes, but my skin was being pulled back so viciously, I could only manage a watery squint.

"I'm lookin' at you! I'm looking at you. Stop it, stop it!" I yelled.

He let my head go with a push, and I immediately put both my hands to my head to massage my scalp to put out the fire that was burning on my head. I naturally turned back toward the front and slumped over.

He grabbed my hair again, jerking my head until half my body was in the back seat.

"DO NOT TURN AWAY FROM ME! DID I TELL YOU TO TURN AROUND? WHAT DO YOU THINK YOU'RE DOING?" he shrieked.

"I'm not doing anything. I just … I don't know what you're talking about."

"Yes, you do know what I'm talking about! You know exactly what I'm talking about. Do you think I'm stupid or something? Answer me!" he demanded.

I saw his face now and it horrified me. It was warped and contorted with anger. I saw the pronounced veins in his forehead expanding and contracting as he yelled.

"No, I, I don't think you're stupid," I stuttered.

My face was wet now with tears.

"You know what? I think you think I'm stupid or something. Look at me when I'm talking to you!"

"I'm looking at you. I'm looking."

"We know what you're doin' and you can't keep an operation like that goin' without cutting us in, understand? You're making money on *our* turf. Who do you think you are? I could kill you right now. I should kill you right now. Whadya think, Jimmy? Should we kill him?

Jimmy said nothing.

The skinny one slapped me again.

"I should kill Paul, too. And his little sister."

He pulled my head back and whispered in my ear. "We've been watching her, you know. She goes to Sheridan Elementary. She goes to school at 8:15 every morning."

With that, he let go, slamming my head into the passenger side window.

"Please let me go. Let me go," I pleaded, wiping my eyes and face of all the tears. "I'm sorry. What do you want me to do?"

I turned back to him and saw clumps of my hair in his hand.

"We oughta kill you right now. How much money you got on you right now?"

"I don't …"

"GIVE ME YOUR MONEY! DO YOU UNDERSTAND ME?" he bellowed, slapping me again.

"Please. I'll give you what I've got. Please."

"Please don't slap you again? Please don't slap you again?" he mocked. "When I'm done wit' you, this guy next to yous gonna put a real beatin' on you."

"No, no. Wha, what do you want from me? What do you want? I don't understand."

"Give me your money. Is that a gold bracelet? Gimme that bracelet."

I took off the gold Gucci bracelet and gave it to him.

"Now what about the watch? Gimme da watch too," he said, motioning impatiently to my wrist.

I had my Movado watch on, but I just couldn't let go of it.

"No, no. It's a knock off," I said. "It's not real. It's fake, it's an imitation. It's not worth anything."

"All right, gimme your money."

I reached in my pocket and shakily pulled the money out of my pocket. It totaled about $300. Stolen, of course.

"Okay, listen up," he said, more calmly this time. The money seemed to have pacified him a little. "Tonight, this is what's gonna to happen. We're gonna go talk to your friend Paul, and we're gonna show him we're serious. And if he tries to go to da police or you try to talk to him before that, we'll come find you and kill you. YOU LISTENIN' TO ME?" He was getting angry again.

"Don't try to tip him off! You understand that, Stupid?"

"Okay, okay, I won't try anything. I promise."

"Good, good. Good for you. Tonight we're gonna meet you. Hollywood Boulevard. The parking lot across the street from

McArthur High School. We're gonna meet you there at nine o'clock tonight. You're gonna be there."

"Yeah, yeah, I'll be there."

"Shut up. This is what we want. Are you listening to me?"

"I'm listening, I'm listening."

"We want $50,000 tonight and $5,000 a month. Do you hear me?"

He grabbed my hair again to make his point.

"Yeah, yeah, I hear you! But I have to go to work. You don't understand. If I don't go to work, nobody's gonna get paid."

"No excuses. Just bring the money tonight. You can't do work on our turf, you understand me? Unless you cut us in."

"Listen, if I don't get to work, I'm gonna be found out. There are checks on my desk. That's evidence against me. If my boss walks over to my desk right now, I will be caught. Nobody'll get money. I'll be arrested."

The linebacker stared straight ahead and said nothing as he lit another cigarette.

"We don't care! Just get us the money. Do you understand that, Stupid?"

"I understand, yeah."

"Good. Now get outta da car."

"What do you mean, 'get out of the car?' I ..."

"What do I mean? What do I mean? I mean get out of the car. That's what I mean. Get outta da car!"

"The car's still running. I ..."

"GET OUT OF THE CAR!"

When I opened the door, they slowed down a little, so when I hit the ground, I rolled a few times but didn't break anything. I looked up from where I lay in the dirt to see my Saab disappear around the curve.

My heart was pounding out of my chest. I felt like I had seen death. I sat for a moment in the dirt on the side of the highway trying to catch my breath. I was still a couple miles from work and had no way to call. I had a car phone in the Saab, but this was before cell phones, so I knew I had no choice but to start walking.

What was I going to tell the people at work? I knew I had to have a good story because my boss, Laurie Sanders, would be there. She trusted me, but I knew she would expect me to call in except under extraordinary circumstances.

At this point, Paul's desires and mine were getting harder and harder to fulfill, so our runs had become almost daily instead of weekly. Because of this, I always had some illegal checks ready to go, just sitting on my desk waiting to be discovered.

I racked my brain, trying to think who could have tipped them off. There's no way Paul could have done this. Then I remembered my conversation with Tommy and Jason at The City Limits, and that their family was rumored to be connected to organized crime. That was the only explanation, but I refused to accept it. They were supposed to be my friends.

Instead of dwelling on that, I focused on how I was going to explain to my boss that I was almost two hours late. Finally, I came up with a reasonably valid excuse. I took the dirt from the highway and rubbed it all over my arms, face, hair, and white button up Guess shirt. I was a clean freak, so it was particularly hard for me to purposely spread germ-ridden dirt all over myself, but these were desperate times.

Almost an hour later, I hobbled into work with my game face on, ready to tell any lie necessary, scared out of my mind. Melvin wasn't at the front desk, so I walked right to Laurie's office. She was on the phone.

"Wait, wait, wait. I'll have to call you right back, okay? Okay, bye," she said, noticing my disheveled state. "What happened? Are you okay?"

"Yeah. The car broke down," I said, letting out a huge sigh.

"Where?"

"Umm, just east of the airport, off Federal Highway. I had the hood open for awhile, trying to … I couldn't figure out what was wrong with it. Finally, I waited for a tow truck and they took it to the shop. I had to walk three miles to get here."

"Oh my goodness, Kevin. That is awful. Why couldn't the tow truck just give you a ride?"

"Oh, the, uh, shop was the other direction. I just decided to walk in. They're going to call me and tell me what the problem is."

"Okay, well, go get cleaned up and go to your desk," Laurie said kindly. "Actually, do you want to go home?"

"No, no, no. I want to work." I knew I had "work" to do cleaning my desk of evidence that would buy me a one-way ticket to the slammer. There would be so many counts against me, I would be federally tried under the RICO Act and sent up the river.

I went to the bathroom to clean up. I felt a bubbling queasiness in the pit of my stomach that just wouldn't go away.

The poverty of my soul was spreading and starting to manifest itself physically in my body. When I looked in the mirror, a vision of myself was revealed to me that, until that moment, was only internal. My dirty, red, battered face, missing hair, and stained clothes were all reflections of my rotting interior. I was, at last, forced to look this visage of my soul squarely in the face.

I didn't like what I saw. It was hideous. The fragile house of cards my ego was built upon was losing its foundation, piece by piece. The crack in the glass was spreading.

My mind was racing. *What should I do? Should I call the police and end this? Should I warn Paul? Should I make a run for it? Should I just listen to what they had told me?*

I decided I had to warn Paul. At lunch, I walked to a pay phone to call him. I don't know exactly why, since I called him every day from work, but somehow this felt different, more dire.

"Paul, you'll never believe what happened." I said frantically. "I, I got abducted. I got ..."

"Kevin, I just got back. I just got beat up," Paul answered calmly. "By the big guy."

"What? What do you mean?"

"Kevin, they told me to tell you that I took your beating."

"What happened?"

"My eyes are black and blue," Paul droned slowly like a zombie. "My lips are bleeding. My nose is broken. And they said that I took your beating. The last words they said to me were unless I cooperate, they're going to kill my sister."

If there was any doubt at all in my mind about the veracity of these guys, this erased it completely.

"Kevin, they wore these gloves with lead in them so it wouldn't make hands marks on my face. They want us to meet tonight."

"I know."

"They want $50,000 tonight and $5,000 a month."

"I know. What are we going to do? We can't get $50,000! We need to buy some time somehow."

"They said they would call me back and let me know exactly the place where we're going to meet."

"Tell them we need another day. We need time to get the money out."

"Okay, I'll tell them," Paul said. I had never heard him sound so scared.

The rest of the day was miserable. I couldn't work. I shuffled papers around for what seemed like hours. People kept coming by and saying they heard my car broke down. I couldn't hide the fact that I was shaken up.

"What's the matter? You never had a car break down before?"

"Not like this I haven't," I answered, trying unsuccessfully to hide my anxiety.

Finally the phone rang at my desk. It was Paul.

"Kevin, we've got an extra day."

"Okay." I breathed a sigh of relief. "I've got a plan. I've got a plan."

"What are we going to do? We don't have that kind of money. We've got to just stop. This is nonsense. I don't want this to happen any longer. I can't take it."

"Listen. I've been thinking. I've got a plan. Let's tell them we don't have the money."

"How're we going to do that?"

"I've got an idea," I whispered. "What if Charles Schwab figures out that Raul Cinfuentes and Ira Cohen have incorrect social security numbers? What if they say we can't release the money or allow you to use the account until you provide correct social security numbers?"

"Hmm. How are we going to prove it?"

"Let me call up the printers for the Sheriff's Office. We have an account with them. Maybe they can print a letter for us."

"You think they'll buy it?" Paul asked incredulously.

"Oh yeah, they'll buy it. It's gonna look real official. Just like the real thing," I said, trying to convince both of us.

"Okay, call me later."

I called over to the printers and a guy picked up on the first ring.

"Hi, this is Kevin Cross. I'm in the Civil Division here at the Sheriff's Office and I've got a question for you. I need you to do a letterhead for me. I need a Charles Schwab letterhead, and the letter needs to say, 'Dear Mr. Cohen, your account has been frozen because we found a problem with your social security number. Until you supply us with a correct social security number, you will not be able to withdraw or make deposits into this account. Sincerely, Charles Schwab.' Something like that. How much would that be?"

"Let me get this straight. You want us to make you one letter with the Charles Schwab logo at the top?"

"Yeah, exactly. We'll give you a copy of the logo."

"We can't do that," he said flatly.

"Oh, ha, it's a gag. It's a birthday party for our friend. We're scaring the guy. It's great, he's my best friend," I stumbled, trying to sound natural. "We're all going to be in on it. It's just an elaborate gag. We just need one. Look, I work for the Sheriff. I can even come in and show you my ID. I mean, c'mon."

"Well, to do one piece of letter, that's gonna cost you as much as $200."

"That's all right. How much will it be exactly?"

"Well ..."

"I need an envelope too. Can you do an envelope for me?"

"Oh, okay. One piece, huh? Let me check."

"Tell you what. I'll make it worth your while. I'll throw in an extra $100 if you can do it for me by tomorrow by 5 P.M."

"Okay, I think we can do that. Come pick it up tomorrow at 5 P.M."

That one piece of letterhead and envelope cost us over $250.

We picked up the envelope and letterhead, and drove to the meet location across from McArthur High School in an abandoned parking lot. It was the first time I had seen Paul since his beating. It was thirty hours or more after the fact, but his face was still a mess. His nose was bruised and jutting off at an angle, both lips were swollen and cut, and his face was full of lacerations. When he saw me, he slowly took off his sunglasses to reveal two giant oval bruises of deep purple and black forming a sac under both of his eyes.

Paul squinted at me through the one eye that was not swollen shut. I saw a sadness and fear in him that sent a shiver through me.

"Paul, I am so sorry. I am so, so sorry. I don't know why they said you took my beating, but ... I am so sorry you did. Whatever it takes, let's just do it. I am so sorry, pal."

I could tell he was angry at me about it. His swollen lips made him slur his words, which made him sound like another person.

"I just want out of this," he said. "I never asked for this, you know? Forget about it. If we get out of this, let's let this be the end. No more."

He paused and looked at me for a second. I could see he wanted to say something important to me, but couldn't form the words. Finally, he gave up and said, "Do you think this'll work?"

"It's going to work, don't worry."

We put the funds that we had not spent into a manila envelope, which amounted to about $8,000 in cash. At that point, we were taking about $2,000-$3,000 per day, but we were spending it almost as fast as it came in. The $8,000 was money from the last few days that we luckily had not yet been able to spend. We thought that would make them happy enough to buy us time to get more cash.

We parked Paul's car across the street and noticed the white stretch limousine sitting in the darkened lot. There was only one streetlight, and the ground was still wet from a light rain. The only other visible lights were the ones emanating from the bottom of the limo.

As we apprehensively approached the limo, the door on the driver's side swung open. The driver popped his head out and motioned to us.

"Over here, fellas. Over here."

*No kidding*, we thought. The only car in an abandoned parking lot is a giant white stretch limo with the motor running. I mean, this is the Mafia. What did they think we were expecting? A Pinto?

The driver got out and opened the door for us. I had seen scenes like this in movies, but never imagined that it would be happening in real life to me. I kept hoping that I would wake up, and it was all just a bad dream.

We got in the back and sat down together. Sitting across from us was an enormous man, who must have weighed at least 300 pounds. He had giant, boil-looking growths all over his face which lent him a monstrous appearance. The only thing that was out of place in this picture was the guy's age. Even through the boils and massive jowls, I could see that he was still young, maybe in his early thirties. He spoke with a heavy Italian accent.

"Eh, guys. Come on in. You met my friends already," he said, motioning to the linebacker, Jimmy, and skinny guy, who were sitting on his right and left. "Come on in, fellas. Can I get you a drink? Whaddya feel like? Whatever you want. You want something?"

"No, that's okay. We don't want anything," I said.

"Okay, guys, whaddya got for us? We don't got much time. We don't wanna rough yous two up again. Paulie boy, you took Kevin's beatin' and you took it like a man, too. Now, Kevin, you gonna do the right thing, or do you wanna get a beatin' yourself? And, and, don't forget about this little girl, this little sister of Paulie. We're gonna cut her up. We're not only gonna take away her innocence, we're gonna cut her up too. You want that, Paulie? You want us to do that to her?"

Paul teared up as they described in detail what they were going to do to the little sister who looked up to him so much.

"No, no, no," I said. "Listen, we've got your money right here."

"Well, good, I'm glad to hear that. You're cooperating. I like that in you guys. You're cooperating, you know. You cooperate, you're gonna be able to make money with us. Listen, you just gotta tell us when you're making money. You gotta do the right thing, guys. You gotta do the right thing. If you don't do the right thing, you're not going to last long. You gotta do the right thing, that's all."

I thought, *You better believe I'm going to do the right thing. I'm out of this business for good.*

As I handed him the envelope, he just stared blankly at me for a moment until the skinny guy snatched it from me.

"How much money you got here?" the boss asked.

"$8,000," Paul said.

"What's this? I thought you was bringing $50,000. Where's the rest of the money? I thought you were gonna cooperate with us, guys. I don't like this. Nope, I don't like this at all."

"Okay, here's the deal," I quickly tried to explain. "We are taking this money from the Sheriff and depositing it into the bank, and we're transferring it to Charles Schwab."

"Yeah, I know, I know. You're making money with Charles Schwab. You're making money all over town and you're not tellin' us. You gotta do the right thing here, boys."

Paul and I exchanged looks. I spoke for us.

"Listen to me for a moment, sir. I'm not going to lie to you. Charles Schwab gave us this letter today when we tried to get the money," I said, taking the letter from my back pocket and handing it to the skinny guy. "They said because we don't have an accurate social security number, they're not going to release the money."

"Gimme the letter. Let me see that." He took the letter in his hands, ripped it up, and threw the shreds at us. "Listen to me. I don't care if you got a letter or not. I don't care if you got a letter from Ronald Reagan himself. We want the money! And, as a matter of fact, we want more money now! You're starting to make me angry."

"Look, we are getting out of this business. We're not going to do this anymore."

"Okay, just give us the money. The $50,000. Give us $50,000 and we'll let you go. You hear me!? Do you wanna take another beating?"

"No, look, look, you don't understand," I stammered.

"Listen, we know how you can get the money. GO STEAL THE MONEY!"

They must have believed us because I know if they didn't, they would have killed us, or at least hurt us badly. Deep down inside I knew these guys were the real criminals and I was just a victim. I was the kid who was really just getting the short end of the stick. I was the kid to feel sorry for. Christian family. Nice boy. Good friends. *These are the bad guys, not me*, I thought.

The big man berated and lectured us, telling us to the do the right thing. He kept saying, "You gotta do the right thing, boys."

I was sitting directly across from him and trying to look directly in his eyes and nothing else.

Suddenly, through the back window of the limo, I saw someone running toward the car. As the man approached the limo, he passed under a street light and I could see his shadowy face. I couldn't believe my eyes. It was Charlie Moreno, the rich guy from my neighborhood that I used to smoke joints with! A feeling of intense nervousness came over me, like acid bubbling in the pit of my stomach, as I tried to wrap my mind around what was happening.

*What was Charlie doing here?* I asked myself. *How could he be connected to these guys? How could Charlie have betrayed us? He didn't even know about our little scheme.*

I discreetly tapped Paul's leg and motioned with my eyes for him to look out the window. Paul's face twisted in recognition. When the skinny guy who had been knocking me around the day before noticed what was happening, he opened the passenger's side door. He stuck his head out and started waving his arms, shouting, "Go! Go! Go back, you idiot!"

Charlie stopped dead in his tracks. I saw his face clearly now, as the streetlamp flooded a yellowish light over half of his face, which looked horribly distorted and full of dread. He turned on his heels and ran, his angular form disappearing hurriedly into a laundromat down the street.

After a few seconds, it dawned on me. The only way Charlie could know about us was through Tommy or Jason. Apparently they were part of the underworld monitoring system that reported everyone who did crime in the Miami area. They got paid for everyone they turned in. We had been betrayed by our closest friends. Charlie couldn't see that we were in the car because of the dark tinted glass, so the thug was trying to keep us from seeing him, since he had orchestrated the brilliant smackdown of the two whiz kids.

Somehow, this knowledge didn't help me understand the situation any better. I thought for a moment that they wouldn't kill us, but then I looked over at Paul and saw his bashed-up face and swollen eyes. I knew they would never let up.

"All right, fellas. It's been real, but the fun's over," the fat one said. "Bring me the $50,000 by tomorrow. My guys will call you and give you instructions. Kevin, you will find your car in front of your apartment. Now get outta my car," he said, dismissing us with a wave of his enormous, flabby arm.

We stepped out of the car without saying a word and walked back across the street to Paul's Trans Am.

"What are we going to do?" Paul asked as we pulled away.

"What can we do? We have to give them the money and tell them we're out of this."

"Let me rephrase that. How are we going to get $42,000 by tomorrow?"

"Well," I sighed. "I've been getting money from accounts that were eight to ten years old, but tomorrow I'll have to find some newer accounts to write checks from. It's risky because if somebody calls up saying, 'I heard I have a refund waiting for me,' the Sheriff's Office is going to tell them, 'We already paid your refund.' They'll look up the check and find it endorsed to Ira Cohen. If it comes to that, it's all over, you know?"

"Yeah, but what choice do we have?"

"None."

The next day I found stale accounts and put checks totaling exactly $41,225 in the usual pile to be approved. Laurie signed off on them, and I got them to Paul during my lunch break. He deposited them equally into the accounts of Raul Cinfuentes and Ira Cohen at Coral Gables Federal like usual.

In the afternoon, Paul called.

"Kevin, there's a problem." My heart immediately froze when I heard Paul's tone.

"What?"

"They're telling me I can't get that kind of money out in one day. We don't have that kind of money. Our branch is too small. If you want to get that kind of cash, you have to call up and tell them you want to withdraw the money."

The drug war was in full swing at this point, and one of the ways police fought the flow of drugs was to control the amount of money that went into and out of banks. The year before, the Miami Federal Reserve Bank had processed more money than every other reserve bank in the United States combined. Whereas a typical bank would process $12 million in funds per day, many Miami banks were processing close to a billion a day. Numerous banks sprung up just to take advantage of the massive influx of drug money.

When the police started to crack down on these banks, legitimate banks toughened their rules as well to avoid being labeled a "drug bank."

"They'll only release $9,000, and then I'll have to put a request in for you to come pick it up tomorrow."

"I have to go there in person?"

"Yeah, you're going to have to. There's no other way."

"Okay, let's give them the $9,000 tonight and tell them we can get them the rest tomorrow. Do you think they'll go for it?" I asked.

"They will. One more thing. When I talked to them, they insisted I go alone."

"Why? Are you sure?"

"Yeah, they were real clear about that," Paul said, clearing his throat. "They want me to go alone."

Paul took the money to them and they gave him instructions that I was to deliver the other $33,000 tomorrow.

The next day I went to Coral Gables Federal to pick up the money on my lunch break. We both decided I couldn't pass for Raul Cinfuentes. I didn't speak Spanish and I had no accent, so I would appear there as Mr. Ira Cohen. Now, in my mind, Mr.

Cohen was much older than twenty, so I wore a little vest with a white shirt and Ray-Ban Wayfarers. My main concern was that they would ask me for ID. I had none.

I identified myself as Ira Cohen to the front desk and waited as a young woman came out to greet me.

"Hello, Mr. Cohen, come right over here," she chirped. "You're here to pick up your cash, is that right?"

"Yes," I said, trying to deepen my voice and use as little words as possible.

"Mr. Johnson, one of our tellers, he's dealt with you a lot?"

"Yes, that's right."

"He's already prepared it all for you. I just need you to sign some forms for me, okay?"

"Okay."

My nerves were on edge, my face must have been flushed, and my heart was heaving itself against my chest so loud that I thought others must be able hear it. Everyone in the bank seemed to be paying attention to me. I was taking out an obscene amount of money. "Please don't ask me for ID," I prayed.

"All right, here we are," she chimed, placing a stack of $100 bills the size of a brick down on the table in front of me. It was more money in one place than I had ever seen before.

"That's it?"

"That's it."

"Well, thank you, Miss …"

"Miss Hollenbeck," she said, pointing to her name tag. "You're so welcome, Mr. Cohen."

"Do you think you could walk me to the car?" I don't know what prompted me to say that. I should have taken the money and run. Now here I was, trying to stay with the bank manager longer than was necessary. I don't know what she would do if something were to happen. I was 150 pounds and she was easily under a hundred pounds. Standing next to each other, we looked like the number 11.

"Why certainly, Mr. Cohen. I'd be delighted to," she said cheerfully, placing her hand on my back and motioning to the door.

I got into the car and took a huge breath, something which I think I had forgotten to do the entire time in the bank. The feeling of relief was incredible. I got away with another one. The boy king rides again.

My orders were to drive to Hallandale Beach Boulevard and head east to the beach. At the beach, I was to go to a hotel called the Hollywood Beach Hilton. I was to come alone, put the money inside a *Wall Street Journal*, go to the eleventh floor, and knock on the door to room 1102.

When I pulled into the parking lot of the Hollywood Beach Hilton, the relief I had felt at getting out of Coral Gables Federal unscathed instantly vanished. I had seen this scene in movies a million times. This is where guys get whacked. You bring them the money, and they take care of you for good.

As I entered the lobby with the newspaper under my arm, I felt the sweat start to come out of the pores on my forehead. I wiped them away with my shirt sleeve and took the elevator to the eleventh floor. I tried to remind myself to breathe, but my mind would not be calm. All I could think about was if these were my last moments alive. Would my last sight be of the Hollywood Beach Hilton? What had my life meant? Was this it? Was life this easy to lose?

The elevator doors opened and I moved onto the eleventh floor. Before I could find room 1102, a door opened at the other end of the hall, and a man I had never seen before walked out and approached me.

"Kevin Cross? You have a newspaper for me?"

"Uh, are you the guy I'm supposed to meet? 1102?" I choked out.

He looked both ways down the hallway. "Is the newspaper exactly as we instructed you?"

"Yeah."

"You are going to stay here for exactly one hour. If you want to live, stay right here. If you follow me, we are going to kill you. And we'll kill Paul and his sister."

"Look, I don't want any problems. I'm out of this. I'm not doing this anymore. Here it is. We're done," I said, handing him the newspaper.

"Do not move," he said calmly, disappearing into the elevator.

I stood in the hallway, not daring to move, for several minutes. Every minute felt like an eternity. I couldn't get the picture out of my mind that they were going to kill me. They had what they wanted. They had no use for me anymore.

After several interminable minutes of waiting in dead silence, I decided I had to get out of there. I dashed for the stairwell and feverishly flew down eleven flights of stairs, sometimes jumping five or six steps at a time, using the rail to steady myself. I got to the bottom of the stairwell and rushed to the exit door. I barely opened the metal door and pressed one eye to the crack, trying to see what kind of car the guy was driving, or if somebody was waiting for me in the parking lot.

I stood there in that stairwell for several minutes, moving my eyeball to try to get a complete picture of the parking lot. I finally realized the coast was clear, so I opened the door to cross the parking lot to my car. I thought running would draw too much attention, so I walked at a normal pace, even though my every emotion was screaming at me to just run for it.

The sound of ambulances and sirens off in the distance filled the air. I wondered if I was going to be next.

# CHAPTER 7

# cheating my way into law school

I got to my car and drove back to my job, penniless and vulnerable. I was petrified. Here I was, clashing against two powers much bigger than myself. One had the power to send me to prison, and the other could kill me on a whim. I didn't know who to be more scared of.

Nick Navarro's administration was known for bending the rules with criminals. Because of the huge-scale drug war raging, law enforcement reverted to tactics more reminiscent of the Wild West. How would they treat me, a guy brazenly stealing money directly from the Sheriff's fund?

Over the next weeks, Monica began to notice my paranoid behavior and asked me why I was acting so strange. I decided to confess everything to her.

"You're a thief?" she said, disgust in her voice.

"Well, technically it's money that no one is going to use. It's just sitting there."

"But is it your money?"

"Well, no. Not exactly."

"And you're buying things with it?"

"Yeah, but ..."

"Hellooo. That's the definition of a thief. But why are you acting so paranoid now? Why are you telling me this now?"

"Sweetie, some local guys found out what we're doing and they wanted us to pay them, that's all. It's all good now. I told them I'm done, not stealing another dime, okay?"

"It's okay? How do you know it's okay? Who are these guys? Should I be scared?"

"I don't know who they are, really. They could be nobody, you know? I'm not sure, honey."

"Nobody? They broke Paul's nose! Do you think these are rational people? You think they're just going to say, 'Oh, you're not going to steal anymore? Well, pleasure doing business with you, have a nice day?' I don't want any part of this!"

"Honey, it's okay. Calm down. Everything is okay. Don't worry. I've got everything under control. I'm going to make everything alright. I know what I'm doing. I'm going to go to law school. Everything I promised you, I will do. I promise. We will go next week and buy that house on Washington that you want. I promise."

"Really? You mean that?" She was enamored with the idea of wealth and affluence. I had learned long before that I could dig myself out of any hole I had dug with her by making promises about a future fairy tale life together.

This should have told me something about her, but I was a serial people-pleaser and had been telling myself, *How can I make this last longer? How can I get this person to like me even more?*

"How about we buy this house and then maybe get married?"

She gasped.

"I'll give you the wedding you always dreamed of. We'll bring your family down and have a big reception, the works. You name it."

"Really?" she said, tears starting to form in the corners of her eyes. "Really, really?"

"Really, my love. You mean the world to me, and I want to give you everything you deserve. I love you with all my heart," I said, putting my arms around her.

"Oh, I love you, too," she choked out between tears. "I love you so much."

The inherent problem with promising her a house and a fantasy wedding was the trifling fact that I was utterly penniless now. The down payment on the house was $20,000, and a nice wedding could equal or surpass that number easily. There was no avoiding it. I would have to go back to the source.

This time, though, I needed all the money. I had to convince the Mafia that I was done stealing, but somehow persuade Paul to steal again and let me keep the lion's share of the money this time. At the time, it seemed only fair. After all, I was taking all the risk. I'm already splitting the money 60-40 with him. He got a nice car out of this, why shouldn't I get a house?

I called Paul up and talked to him for sixty emotional minutes, using every trick in the book to persuade him:

"C'mon, man, we've been pals since elementary school."

"It's not for me, it's for Monica. I already promised her."

"You got a nice car when I just fixed mine up."

"I would do it for you."

"The guys are off our back. We paid them off. We don't need to worry about anything anymore."

"We'll be more careful."

"I'll make it up to you. I'm going to go to law school and I'll be in a position to help you."

I begged, pleaded, and groveled until he finally caved. We agreed we would do a few more transactions, and after that, it would be over.

After that call, our friendship was as good as dead. It had been deteriorating for months, and Paul was beginning to feel slighted because I was taking more of the money than he was getting. He had come to me a couple months before this, telling me he wanted more money or he would stop depositing the checks. In a moment of anger, he even threatened to end it and turn me in.

"I could take a plea bargain and never do any time, you know that right?" he bellowed.

Over the next month, I carefully culled money from every stale account I could find, sometimes even dipping into dangerously recent ones. I gathered enough for my needs and we made our last deposits and withdrawals without a problem. We were done. We had gotten away with it relatively unscathed. The Sheriff's Office and Coral Gables Federal were none the wiser, the mob guys were satisfied that I was done stealing, and we still had all the stuff we bought with the funny money.

I decided I had narrowly averted disaster and now I would do everything above board. I had even lined up some part-time work doing the books for my new wave hairdresser, a guy named Scott Padova. Scott was a nice guy, but couldn't go an hour without using cocaine. He would leave his customers mid-cut to go to the bathroom for a snort, emerging a few minutes later, chattering away, full of nervous energy. I sat in a back room doing his books and he would pop his head in every once in awhile to ask how I was doing, but never stayed long enough for an answer.

I put a $20,000 down payment on the house on Washington Street and got a forty-year negative amortization loan. My monthly payment was less than what was necessary to even pay for interest, so after ten years, I would actually owe more on the house than when I started. For a so-called financial investment genius, I was pretty dumb.

The stuff we had in the old apartment wasn't good enough to move into a new home, so we filled our abode with chrome, Lucite, glass, red leather sofa sets, and pieces of modern art fashioned out of chicken wire. We bought a turquoise and pink couch made out of the back of a Ford for $1,500, and spent thousands on the floors to give the house a *Miami Vice* Art Deco look. Monica and I settled in and started planning for the wedding of our dreams.

I rented a decadent yacht for $10,000, hired a popular DJ, paid for an exclusive chef and a carving station, bought top shelf liquor, and purchased an obscenely extravagant dress for Monica. The wedding was a magnificent offering to the gods of debauchery that would have made Caligula blush.

As expected, everyone at the wedding got drunk and disorderly. Every half hour or so, Scott Padova would lead a progression of people to the bathroom to indulge in his drug of choice. Scott and I were doing exactly the same thing, only my addiction was to an empty lifestyle of endless spending and anesthetizing my heart with money. I could use my drug out in the open and even be lauded for it.

Six months earlier, I was studying for the Law School Aptitude Test (LSAT). My plan was to get into St. Thomas Law School, a prestigious law school in South Florida. My undergraduate grades were pretty average, so I had been studying for over a year and decided to take a refresher course as the day of the test neared. My study partner, Jason Cranton, was a fastidious worker. He was going to the test preparation school every day while I was going one night a week.

When test day arrived, Mr. Cranton and I sat next to each other due to the proximity of our last names. It didn't matter though, because it's hard to cheat on that exam because everyone gets a different test. I could be working on section one while he is working on section five.

A moral dilemma raged in my mind. I had been drinking the night before and knew I wasn't at my best. Should I just give it my best shot and hope for the best, or should I take matters into my own hands? One phrase kept repeating in my head, *I've got to get into law school. I've got to get into law school. I've got to.*

I looked around the room at the hundreds of other students furiously writing. *I deserve to be here just as much as these guys do,* I reasoned. *I have to work for a living, though. I don't have the time to waste spending every day studying, but I know I'm capable.*

I knew I couldn't ask God for help. I knew He wasn't listening, and even if He was, why would He help me, anyway?

I resolved to cheat, and tried to sneak a peek at Jason Cranton's paper many times, but to no avail. Then I got to a section called "Logic Games." When I sneaked a peek this time, I could tell he was working on the same section. It didn't take me long to realize that I was not going to pass "Logic Games." The section had a one hour time limit and they gave us two minutes each to answer the most mind-bending questions I had ever encountered.

I answered a few on my own, but then followed his answers for the rest. Amazingly, the next two sections went the same way. The last section was for testing sample purposes, so I guessed I didn't have to do well on that one. I guessed correctly. I ended up getting a 36, the highest grade in the school where I had applied. Incredibly, I got a perfect score on one section, "Logic Games." As a result, I was offered a half-scholarship to St. Thomas Law School in Miami Gardens. They said, "Well, Mr. Cross, your grades in Undergraduate at Nova aren't very good, but we see you can do it with the LSAT."

It never dawned on me at the time that all of my so-called "successes" were actually the result of lying, cheating, and stealing. My ego soared as if the accomplishments were my own. To my friends and family and the outside world, they were, and that's all that mattered.

In order to give my full attention to school, I had to quit the job at the Sheriff's Office. They threw me a big going away party with cake and balloons, and everyone congratulated me and gave me cards. Most said, "We can't wait to have you back here someday as a lawyer."

I was relieved to leave there scot-free, with my reputation still intact. I had scammed everybody and had gotten away with it. Now, with me gone and a new guy taking over my position, there was virtually no way to trace anything back to me from the accounts. I had erased any clue to the pilfered accounts from the hard drives and the reports.

Without the job, I could convincingly tell the Mafia guys I was not stealing anymore. They knew I couldn't keep embezzling if I wasn't employed there, so I was no longer "working on their turf." I'm sure the Tomeleri brothers verified my story, so I was off the hook with them. If they bumped me off, Sheriff Navarro and the FBI would certainly conduct an investigation, and the trail might lead them back to the mob. It was trouble they couldn't risk. These guys had bigger people than me to go after, and as long as I stayed out of their sight, they wouldn't mess with me.

Monica was distracted with the new home and believed my troubles were over. I believed it, too, to some degree, but I still couldn't completely relax. I was constantly looking over my shoulder, and always had an escape route planned, just in case.

When I started law school in the fall, I was scared to death. The old saying about law school is that they scare you to death the first year, work you to death the second year, and bore you to death the third. This was certainly the truth for me. I was petrified.

I went from being a high roller to a starving student with a mortgage to pay. I worshiped at the altar of new gods, ones that were fashioned out of plastic and adorned in gold, platinum, and silver. The new gods were a step up from my old gods, or so I thought. The "gods of credit" let me do the same things I did before and live the same grand lifestyle, but they allowed me to do it legally. These were merciful gods.

"You don't have the money to pay us? It's okay, don't worry. You don't have to now. Just wait. Give us a small offering and you're off the hook. Love ya!" the credit cards sung to me cheerfully.

I worshiped them every day without fail. In return, they unfailingly helped me out of every situation I found myself in. I didn't even have to pray to them. I worshiped them to the tune of $50,000 while paying my mortgage, buying all the stuff that made me happy, and paying for the rest of my schooling. I also took advantage of borrowing the maximum in student loans to pay for essentials like books, alcohol, drugs, and junk for the Saab.

I found other ways to make cash, too. During my first semester, I met two guys at the law school: one an Italian whose dad was "connected," and the other a Jewish guy who had ties with a Jewish Mafia in the Miami area. I don't know how I attract these people, but somehow I was a magnet for organized crime of all races and creeds.

They came to me one day and said, "Kid, you wanna make some money?"

"Yeah, I wanna make money. What do you think I'm here for? I love money. I just kind of ran into some hard times. I've got a house now. Got to make payments. I've gotta buckle down, live on credit cards. You know what I'm saying, right?"

"Kid, you could make $200 a week doing our homework. What do you think?"

"Are you kidding? Legal research? I'm in. Bring it on, baby."

It felt good to have cold hard cash in my hands again. I knew I had to buckle down and study, though, because I wanted to make money. The only way I saw to make money was to finish law school and maybe go to the FBI.

Or maybe not. Maybe I could just hang out with these connected guys and work with them. The Law Firm of Dewey, Cheatum, and Howe. I could be the brains of the operation. They could do all the wise guy stuff, I would be the genius raking in the money in the background.

The weeks turned into months. Trying to put my past life behind me, I plugged away in law school, earning decent grades and enjoying an improving relationship with Monica. My life was back on track until February 10, 1988.

It was a brisk Tuesday, and like all Tuesdays, Monica and I were cuddling and watching a movie together. Around eight o'clock, I heard a loud knocking at the door. Monica looked at me with vague concern.

"Who could that be? We aren't expecting anyone," she said.

I got up from the couch and peeked out the window. Bright red and blue lights were flashing from the back of the house.

*No! This can't be,* I thought. *How could they have found out? I covered my tracks so well.*

The day that I was convinced would never come was here.

# CHAPTER 8

# in the belly of the whale

"Who is it?" I asked.

"FBI and Broward Sheriff's Office. Open up," a voice replied from the other side of my front door.

I cautiously cracked open the door. An FBI agent and three Broward County Police officers were standing on my front step. The one closest to me pushed the door open all the way.

"Raymond Kevin Cross?"

"Yeah?"

"You have the right to remain silent and refuse to answer questions. Do you understand this?" he said, spinning me around and pushing me against the wall. I offered no resistance.

"Yes." I was almost relieved at the finality of what was happening. It was finally over.

Monica was screaming.

"Anything you say or do may be used against you in a court of law. Do you understand this?" he said, slapping the handcuffs on my wrists and cinching them tightly.

"Yes."

"What are you doing? What's going on? He hasn't done anything wrong!" Monica shrieked.

"You have the right to an attorney present during questioning. If you cannot afford an attorney, one will be appointed for you. Do you understand these rights?"

I didn't have a belt on and the officer put the handcuffs through the belt loop on the back of my pants, so the front part of my jeans was falling down.

"Do you understand?"

"Yes, I do. Monica, don't worry. I'll be back. Stop screaming. It's okay."

"If you decide to answer questions now without an attorney present, you will still have the right to stop answering at any time until you talk to an attorney. Do you understand?"

"Yeah. I don't have any shoes. Can I get some shoes?"

At this, one of the officers went to my bedroom and returned with an expensive pair of Italian loafers. The irony hit me immediately when I saw them. I had seen them at a trendy downtown boutique and lusted after them for weeks, finally covering the $250 price tag with my credit card. They fit me in the store that day, but never again. They sat in the closet, unused, for months. Now they finally had a purpose; to carry me to jail.

"Do you understand the rights I have just read to you? With these rights in mind, do you wish to speak to me?"

"I need to talk to a lawyer." I was only in my second semester of law school, but I knew enough to always ask for a lawyer.

I slid on the loose fitting loafers and they walked me to the car.

"Watch your head, son," the escorting officer told me, putting his hand on the top of my head and guiding me into the back seat. The stench of old metal from the cage separating the front and back seats filled my nostrils as the door slammed shut behind me.

Everything around me was bathed in brilliant alternating blues and reds. I sat in the car alone for a moment, trying to get oriented. Every few seconds, the radio inside the car would crackle and some unintelligible stream of words would break the silence. I moved my position to try to see what was going on. Two policemen were attempting to calm Monica down, and the FBI agent and another officer were discussing something a few feet from my door.

These last moments were too sudden and jarring to feel real to me. Of course, I knew I was experiencing it. Everything was tangible there—the sound of the radio, the flashing lights, the smell inside the patrol car—but from my vantage point, it all felt other-worldly. It didn't feel like a dream. It felt like another universe.

Eventually, two officers got into the front seat and we pulled away from the house. I watched as Monica faded away, standing on the sidewalk in her pink silk pajamas, crying.

The cop who wasn't driving turned around in his seat to address me.

"So you're the guy who's been stealing all the money." He said it calmly and deliberately, but with obvious menace in his voice.

"Guys, I, I need to talk to a lawyer."

"Don't worry, you'll talk to a lawyer. But you're going to talk to us first."

I was sitting on my handcuffs and they kept getting tighter, digging into my skin and causing me incredible pain. I maneuvered myself so I was sitting sideways with my head against the passenger side window and my feet touching the driver's side door.

"Can you please loosen my handcuffs?"

"We know everything. We know how you did it. We know everything, kid."

"Just a little. Please. They're cutting my wrists. I think I'm bleeding."

"It's okay. You're gonna be fine."

"No, please, just loosen them a little. I'm …"

"Nope, you're fine."

I begged and pleaded with them the entire ride, but they never relented. First, they took me to my old office. Not exactly to my office, but the same building where I had worked every day. They led me into what looked like a cafeteria and sat me down in one of the chairs. The room was completely dark save for one florescent bulb that flashed on and off intermittently. All the chairs were sitting, legs up, on the rows of picnic-style tables. Another officer came in and put shackles on my legs. By now, it was around 10 P.M. and I was dead tired.

"Okay, kid."

"Please, unlock the cuffs a little. Please."

"Depends. You going to talk to us?"

"Okay, yeah, yeah. I'll talk to you. Just take the cuffs off."

They finally unlocked them and put them down on the table in front of me.

"Okay, so tell us what happened. Tell us about the money you stole. Tell us about all of the money. We know exactly what you did. Now we want to know who you're in with, what you're doing, everything."

"You know what? With all due respect, I'm in law school and what they taught us is you ask for a lawyer first."

"Son, you're gonna have plenty of time to talk to a lawyer. Right now, you need to talk to us."

"With all due respect, sirs, I need to talk to a lawyer."

"All right. You got it. But we ain't gonna be so nice next time, comprende?"

They left me in the cafeteria all night. Every half an hour, they would come back in and ask if I was ready to talk.

"Sir, I need to talk to a lawyer."

Then they would leave and I would be alone with my thoughts for a little while until they tried again. All I could think about was that I needed to talk to Paul before they could get to him. If I could get to Paul, I could tell him, "Don't squeal! They've got nothing on us. Nobody can prove we took the money. There's not even one shred of physical evidence."

"Are you ready to talk to us now, boy?" They kept prodding. "It'll be much easier for you if you just talk to us now."

This went on all night. Finally, they put the handcuffs back on and drove me to the jail. As we approached, a massive gate swung open and then shut behind us with a loud rattle. Then another set of gates opened in front of us as we pulled up to the entrance.

They took me inside, fingerprinted me, and threw me in a holding cell with a bunch of other guys sleeping off hangovers, or waiting for someone to pick them up. Some of the guys knew each other, so I imagined there must be a whole community of drunks passing through every night of the week in these filthy digs.

After an hour or so, they called my name and took me to a private room where a man was waiting for me. On his hands he wore rubber gloves, and on his face, a disgruntled look.

"Hello. How are you?" I asked.

"Remove everything from your pockets and place them on the table."

"I don't have anything in my pockets."

He put his hand in all my pockets and dug around to make sure.

"Remove all your clothing, one piece at a time. Keep your hands in my sight at all times, you understand? When you are done removing a piece of clothing, place it on the table."

"Yes sir," I said, complying with his request. When I was done, he searched through my clothes while I stood naked.

When he was satisfied that I had nothing in my clothes, he turned his attention to me. He first ran his fingers through my hair and then told me to tilt my head back as he looked in my nostrils.

"Open your mouth nice and wide. That's good. Now lift up your tongue. Okay, now pull your upper lip up. Now your lower lip. Good."

He grabbed my head and turned it both ways, checking in and behind my ears.

"Place both your arms in the air and turn around full circle," he said mechanically. "Now I want you to squat on the floor and cough. Do that now."

I obeyed, shamed and humiliated. Finally, he allowed me to put my clothes back on, and they escorted me to a place where I was issued a tan polyester and cotton shirt with matching pants.

"Take off your clothes and put these on."

They took my clothes, placed them in a tan bag, and wrote on it: "Cross, Raymond Kevin" and the number "5207593-40." The woman behind the desk handed me a bar of soap, a comb, and a toothbrush.

"Do not lose these," she said dryly.

I was then led through a seemingly endless labyrinth of corridors until we reached what they call a "pod." The door slid open to reveal a huge round room constructed almost entirely of bulletproof glass. There were two levels: the lower level, a wide open space with picnic tables and a single TV blaring unintelligibly above the cacophony, and the upper level, which was all doors and a catwalk. The floors resembled the material used to make basketball courts, and so every sound in the place reverberated. The resulting effect was deafening.

The jail itself was maximum security and had just been built in 1985 for $41.6 million, so it was relatively clean. It was the crowning achievement of the Navarro administration.

In the lower level, about fifty men milled about, some playing cards, some yelling loudly, others trying to watch TV. When I walked in, everyone turned to look at me, and the already deafening sound level increased with the profanity and jeers aimed in my direction. I glanced at their sneering faces and was petrified.

One of the officers turned to me.

"You're up there," he said, laughing and motioning to the upper level with his head. "Room number five."

I couldn't figure out why they were laughing, but I knew it wasn't good.

"That's the 'Wendy's murderer' up there. He's your cellmate. Hope you enjoy your stay with us."

"I need to be put in solitary confinement. You don't understand. I worked for the Sheriff. I'm in law school. I'm, I'm white collar, I have … I'm practically a lawyer. You can't put me in here with these criminals," I pleaded as they turned and closed the door in my face.

I just stood there in a daze for a few seconds as every eye in the whole pod was on me. I looked at the floor and said nothing. I didn't want anyone to know who I was.

I was exhausted and my head was pounding, so I decided to go up to my room. Avoiding eye contact at all cost, I shuffled up the stairs with my head down and found room five. The door was open and a kid who appeared to be my age was sitting on the corner of his bunk. The cell had two bunks along the left and back wall that formed an L, and a toilet made of stainless steel with no seat. Each bed had a mattress and gray blanket, but no pillows.

The guy didn't make eye contact with me as I entered, and we made no acknowledgement of each other. But I knew who he was. Everyone in South Florida knew who Bernell Hegwood was.

On May 23, 1987, Bernell walked into the Wendy's fast-food restaurant in Fort Lauderdale where he worked, and shot and killed a manager and two fellow employees. He took $1,700 from the safe and fled with his girlfriend to Louisiana. His mother, Annie Broadway, who worked at the same Wendy's, came forward to the police three days later, telling them her son had confessed to the murders and robbery. She collected a $36,000 reward from Wendy's for giving her son up.

When police caught up to him five days later, in his possession he had a considerable amount of cash, clothing, and jewelry that he had bought for himself and his girlfriend. The trial started in January and it only took one month for the jury to find Hegwood guilty of armed robbery and three counts of murder.

The day I entered the jail, February 10, 1988, Bernell had received his verdict of three death sentences. We said nothing to each other. I came in and put down my soap, toothbrush, and comb, and sat on the corner of my bed.

I was numb. How did I end up here? It couldn't just be fate, or luck, or destiny, or karma. If that was true, if our lives are just battered about randomly by an unseen, indifferent force, it was too depressing to go on. The thought that our only purpose and chance for satisfaction in this accidental life is to stockpile stuff was debilitating to me.

I had tried those things that are supposed to bring satisfaction. I lived the "good life." I had the money, the house, the car, the girl, and I still wondered, "Is this all?" All those things only left me a vacant husk of a human being sitting in a prison cell, penniless and alone.

I thought about my life and broke it down, trying to figure out what I knew for sure:

I knew that the way I was doing things was not working.

I knew that I could not accept the fact that our lives were a meaningless race to pack in as much pleasure as possible.

I knew that something, or someone, was trying to get my attention. And I knew that whoever, or whatever, finally had it.

My thoughts were interrupted by the call for breakfast. Bernell and I got up from our beds and made our way to the dining area. I tried my best to not be noticed, but as soon as I got to the bottom of the stairs, a guy who looked about twenty years older than me and a hundred pounds heavier, all tattooed muscle, put his arm around me.

"Yo, what're you down for, kid?"

"Me? Down for? I dunno. What do you mean?"

"You know. What'd ya do? Rob, steal, kill? It's in that vein."

"Oh, me? I … nothing, really. I, I stole some money."

"No kidding? Me, too. Got me up on armed robbery and aggravated assault or somethin'. I didn't do it though. Been in here a year 'cause I heard somethin' my old cellmate said, and now they got me testifying on this case. I'm Calvin. How you doing?"

"I'm okay. I'm Kevin," I muttered, trying to be friendly, but not too friendly. I didn't want to be seen as more than a friend to him.

"Hmm. Well, listen, you're about to have the worst breakfast of your miserable life. I promise you that. Don't give it to nobody, though, 'cause you'll be giving it to somebody every day if you do. Don't do it kid. I got my eye on you," he warned as we got our trays.

The breakfast consisted of the following:

    1 slice of white bread

    1 ice-cream scoop of a yellow egg-like material

    1 scoop of grits

    1 brick of brown, mangled hash browns

    1 cup of coffee from giant brown plastic bins

    1 juice cup with a foil lid

I found out that the prisoners liked to save the juice cups. They'd use them to fashion little boiler pots with handles that would grip the light socket in their cells to make alcohol.

I took my tray and tried to find a place to sit down. It felt like grade school all over again. This time, though, the bullies were much larger, and they weren't after your lunch money.

I sat down and stared at my breakfast. My anxiety had taken my appetite away. Even if I did have an appetite, I think this breakfast would have ruined it.

Calvin came by with his tray in hand.

"Yo, Kev, my main holly bally squally. You gonna eat that? Can I have it?"

I found out that Calvin's favorite phrase was "holly bally squally." He used it for everything; it was a nickname for people he liked, it was a way to say hello, a way to say goodbye, an expression of frustration, and a cry of joy.

"Well, yeah, I guess so. I can't eat," I moaned.

He balanced his tray in one hand, put the foil-topped juice cup in his mouth, grabbed my tray with his free hand, and walked away with my breakfast.

I started to walk back to my room with an aching hunger in my belly. This was the worst hunger I had ever felt. It wasn't for food though. It was a hunger for something that could satisfy me. I hoped it existed.

On the back wall I noticed a bookshelf with the usual donated jailhouse books: worn out copies of cheesy suspense novels, the

*I'm OK, You're OK* self-help books, coverless classics edited by inmates to include profanity and obscenities, copies of *The Watchtower,* and tattered pieces of every version of the Bible ever written. I hated reading novels and I didn't need any Zig Ziglar, so I picked up one of the Bibles and took it back to the room with me.

Now, I was well aware of the two options for imprisoned folks:

1. Become immersed in the law to the point of being able to pass the bar, reading everything you can get your hands on in an attempt to save your hide.

2. Find God, become immersed in the Bible to the point of being able to pass seminary, reading everything you can get your hands on in a selfish attempt to save your hide.

I didn't care about any conversion. I just wanted to get my mind off my situation. This book was in terrible condition, with major portions ripped and torn, but I turned randomly to a chapter in the Book of Matthew. My eyes feel on this passage spoken by Jesus:

> *Are you tired? Worn out? Burned out on religion? Come to me. Get away with me and you'll recover your life. I'll show you how to take a real rest. Walk with me and work with me—watch how I do it. Learn the unforced rhythms of grace. I won't lay anything heavy or ill-fitting on you. Keep company with me and you'll learn to live freely and lightly.* (Matthew 11:28-30, MSG)

This came as a revelation to me. The God of my childhood, the God of rules and regulations, of fire and brimstone, wanted me to live freely and lightly? At Christian school, God was never taught as a friend. At church I remember saying, "Yeah, yeah, God loves me, but what does that do for me right now?"

I found no practical connection to my life in the words of my parents, or teachers, or pastors. Now, reading a torn and dirty

Bible on my cell bunk, the words finally meant something to me. I wanted to recover my life.

I tried to sleep for awhile, but couldn't. I decided to use the phone. I got up and waited in line, keeping my head down to avoid any trouble. When it was my turn, I dialed Monica.

"Hello?"

"Hi. It's me."

"Kevin?" I heard Monica say anxiously, with a crack in her voice. "Are you okay? What's going on? Where are you?"

"Honey, I'm in jail. I can only talk for a few minutes. Listen to me. I have to get out of here. Call my parents and tell them I need a lawyer. A good one. Okay?"

"Okay, I will. Are you going to be okay? What are they doing to you? What am I supposed to do?" she said, her voice quivering.

"Just get me out of here. Get me out of here. Call my parents and get a lawyer."

"Okay. I love you."

"Love you, too."

I hung up the phone and looked behind me. There was no one waiting. I knew my mom would be at home, so I called her collect.

"Mom, I'm in jail and you need to get me out of here. I have to get out of this place," I said, trying to fight the tears welling up in my eyes at the sound of her voice.

"Honey, I will do everything I can. Are you okay?"

"Mom, just get me out ..." I couldn't finish the sentence as I started to cry.

I heard my mother sobbing on the other end. Hearing her crying was more than I could take. I turned my back on the pod, covered my face with my arm, and wept.

"We'll ... do what ... ever it ... takes," she choked through her tears.

"Please, mom. Please. Get me out of here. Please."

I got a call in the afternoon that I had a visitor. The guards escorted me to a vacant room with an old table and two chairs. I waited for a few minutes, and finally the door opened.

A guy I didn't recognize walked in and set his battered briefcase on the table. His jean jacket and faded jeans made him look like a classic draft dodger. He sported a big gray, unkempt beard, and his scraggly hair was tied back in a pony tail. I could smell a little body odor when he approached me to shake hands.

"I'm Howard Bernstein, your public defender. How are you, Mr. Cross?"

"I've had better days."

"Okay, let me get this straight," he said, looking down at a piece of paper he had pulled from his briefcase. You went to a Christian school and you stole money? Hundreds of thousands of it?"

"Yeah, that's true."

"I brought you some water," he said, handing me a cup of cold water. "Okay, so you made up two fake names on the accounts you deposited into, right? Ira Cohen, and uh, let's see, Raul Cinfuentes. Is that correct?"

"Yes, that's true."

"So you're a Christian kid who didn't learn his lesson, and then you decided to pick on the Jewish people and the Cubans. Typical," he scoffed.

"That has nothing to do with anything. You've got it all wrong. What are you talking about?" I asked.

*What have I done*, I thought. Not only was I in trouble and under arrest, but I was realizing there would be a ripple effect that I hadn't bargained for.

"I think we're done here."

"Already? That's it?"

"I'm going to talk to the judge and get your bail lowered. $500,000 is ridiculous. We'll get it lowered and I'll be in touch. Have a good one, Kevin."

With that, he grabbed his briefcase, paused for second looking me in the eye, and then disappeared out the door. I had to get a new lawyer.

I returned to the pod and spent the rest of the day wandering aimlessly, playing spades with Calvin and other guys, reading the Bible, listening to disgusting prison stories, and thinking about the mess I was in. I learned that Calvin was the de facto leader of the pod and most of the inmates listened to and respected him. He seemed to take a liking to me, so I tried to respond in kind and humor him. Everyone wanted to know what I did, but I tried to hold back as many details as I could while trying not to arouse any anger.

The verse I had read earlier stayed in the back of my mind. Something about it calmed me and gave me a tangible peace and hope for my life that I had not felt for a long time. When the call finally came to go to bed, I anxiously returned to the tattered Bible.

The Wendy's murderer was sleeping in his bed against the left wall, so I lay down on the bed away from my cellmate facing the back wall. I didn't know what was worse, facing him or not facing him. I didn't know what emotional state he would be in after murdering three people, and then finding out that very day that he had been sentenced to death. I had visions of him murdering me in the middle of the night. I was more scared, though, of what was going to happen to me in the coming weeks.

It was freezing cold in the cell. All I had to keep warm was a hospital blanket, so I covered myself with it as best I could. I picked up the Bible and turned to the Book of Timothy, where I read a passage that seemed as if it had been written directly to me:

*For we brought nothing into the world, and we can take nothing out of it. But if we have food and clothing, we will be content with that. People who want to get rich fall into temptation and a trap and into many foolish and harmful desires that plunge men into ruin and destruction.*

*For the love of money is a root of all kinds of evil. Some people, eager for money, have wandered from the faith and pierced themselves with many griefs.* (1 Timothy 6:7-10)

Every word rang true for me. When I was growing up, reading the Bible was always a monotonous affair. It was all empty, meaningless words written by old prophets dealing with a completely different set of problems. I would read it to please my parents, or to get a candy from the Sunday school teacher for reciting it. I never realized until that moment that the Bible had wisdom that actually applied to what I was going through. I read on:

*But you, man of God, flee from all this, and pursue righteousness, godliness, faith, love, endurance and gentleness. Fight the good fight of the faith.... Command those who are rich in this present world not to be arrogant or to put their hope in wealth, which is so uncertain, but to put their hope in God, who richly provides us with everything for our enjoyment. Command them to do good, to be rich in good deeds, and to be generous and willing to share. In this way they will lay up treasure for themselves as a firm foundation for the coming age, so that they may take hold of the life that is truly life.* (1 Timothy 6:11-12, 17-19)

*The life that is truly life?* I thought. I wanted that. Nothing I had tried felt like anything even approximating true life. It was more like a movie set full of elaborately decorated facades that would fall with the slightest nudge and reveal the nothingness behind it.

There was no way to rationalize or sugarcoat it: I was incredibly arrogant and had put my faith in a wealth which had left me in a matter of hours. It turned its heels and ran at the first sign of sorrow. But this verse said that God was promising to provide everything for my enjoyment. I had experienced the pleasures of this world, but the enjoyment lasted about as long as a bite of cotton candy.

I turned to the verse I had read earlier that day and read it again. I found incredible solace in it. A peace came over me that words cannot do justice to. I had to read it one more time:

*Are you tired? Worn out? Burned out on religion? Come to me. Get away with me and you'll recover your life. I'll show you how to take a real rest. Walk with me and work with me—watch how I do it. Learn the unforced rhythms of my grace. I won't lay anything heavy or ill-fitting on you. Keep company with me and you'll learn to live freely and lightly.*

As I read the words, I couldn't fight back the tears. I lay there in bed, shivering, quietly crying, and trying my best to hide my sniffs and breaths for air. Each tear that dropped took with it a great burden I had been carrying on my back for years. My spirit lifted as I decided I would try to connect with God.

I thought God was mad at me and I didn't know how to start talking to Him. It's like being in a room alone with someone you have wronged. Going up to them and saying, "Gee, I'm really sorry" doesn't mean a thing. I just started talking, hoping He would understand:

"Well, I guess it's just you and me now, God. I don't know if you want to talk to me or zap me. I know saying sorry isn't good enough. I know I have been doing things my way. I have no peace. I have no hope. I can't find any peace. If you can hear me, if you are there, please forgive me. Can you give me peace? I don't have it and I could really use it right now. Will you give me peace, please? I'm begging you. I want your peace. I want a life that is true life," I pleaded through my sobs and shivers. "I'm sorry, I'm sorry, I'm sorry, I'm really, really sorry, God." And I meant every word.

At that point, my relief was so great that the floodgates just burst. My emotions were too strong to hold back. The tears of pity for my own situation transformed into tears of pure joy, and I couldn't hide it. I'm sure Bernell must have heard my weeping, but he remained still in his bed.

I lay awake for an hour or so, reading the Book of Psalms. I read David's prayer to God after committing adultery with Bathsheba:

> *Have mercy on me, O God, according to your unfailing love; according to your great compassion blot out my transgressions. Wash away all my iniquity and cleanse me from my sin. For I know my transgressions, and my sin is always before me. Against you, you only, have I sinned and done what is evil in your sight, so that you are proved right when you speak and justified when you judge.* (Psalm 51:1-4)

I slept intermittently that night, so when the call for breakfast came at 7 A.M., I was already awake. I was served the same breakfast as the day before and actually ate some of it, my first sustenance for at least thirty hours. After breakfast, I went to the phone and called my mother. The television was blaring in the background, so it was nearly impossible to carry on a conversation.

Suddenly, I heard a roar coming from other prisoners behind me. I turned around to see what the commotion was all about, only to see my face on the TV. The local news was telling everyone in the room what I had done. I had already told some of these guys that I had stolen, but I didn't tell them from whom. This jail was built by Nick Navarro. I worked for Nick Navarro. And now they knew I had stolen from Nick Navarro.

There were two types of people in this jail. One group didn't have a problem with law enforcement, but didn't like Nick Navarro in particular and would do anything to get out. The other, the majority, didn't like anyone even associated with the police or law enforcement, and would do anything to get retribution. I prayed they were the former.

All the inmates started banging the plates, cups, books, and anything they could make noise with. It was all directed at the mug shot of me on the screen. Ann Bishop and Dwight Lauderdale from Channel 10 News were delivering the story to all of South Florida about the young kid who had fleeced the most powerful sheriff in Florida, maybe in the country.

"... Paul then cashed the checks at the 163rd Street Mall's branch of Coral Gables Federal where he worked as a teller. In all, the two stole close to $300,000. Mr. Cross was picked up late Wednesday night at his home in Hollywood after an anonymous tip turned him in," the TV reporter said, showing a mug shot of my best friend Paul next to mine.

Until then, I didn't know where Paul was, or if he had been arrested as well. I knew now that it really was all over.

The ruckus got louder and louder, and the mob started to move towards me. I didn't know what to do. Did this horde think that I was the sheriff, and would they try to take their rage out on me? I put down the phone and uttered a quick prayer in my head. Not just a jailhouse, get-me-out-of-here prayer. I said, "Please protect me. Give me your words."

The television report continued, "... seen here on surveillance video from Coral Gables Federal, where Mr. Cross entered on June 17 of last year to withdraw a sum of $41,225 under the pseudonym of Ira Cohen."

They were getting closer and more frenzied. I couldn't gauge from their faces whether this was hatred or adulation.

"... A graduate of Florida Bible Christian School, Nova University, and current student at St. Thomas Law School in Miami Gardens ...," the TV blared.

*Please don't let them take it out on me!* I pleaded inside.

When story ended, every eye in the place focused on me. Everyone who was not already coming my direction, turned and joined the other inmates who were starting to encircle me. I hung up the phone and asked myself, *Do I run to the door and scream for the guards?*

Before I could figure out what to do to get out of there, the unexpected happened. Calvin started a cheer that flooded through the prison, "Kev-in, Kev-in, Kev-in."

Soon the whole pod was cheering in unison. All the sneers and jeers transformed into smiles.

"Kev-in, Kev-in, Kev-in, Kev-in."

The clamor got louder and louder as they crowded around me. I sheepishly smiled, not enjoying the attention, but was relieved that they weren't going to kill me.

Everyone crowded around, questioning me about every sordid detail. From that moment on, I enjoyed a celebrity status among most of the prisoners of pod #3.

It was a precarious position I found myself in, though. I was being exalted and revered by men who were rapists, murderers, gang members, a host of drug dealers, and even child molesters. But I found that my increased visibility and movement up the hierarchal rank also welcomed the wrath and jealousy of those now "beneath" me. I became a hero and a target all at once.

The week passed more rapidly, as I was discovering a new purpose for my life. I felt I had already thrown away my twenty years of life and I could not afford to waste another minute. I spent my days in the cell devouring everything about God I could get my hands on. I feasted on everything, even books that seemed like utter nonsense to me. Whenever I found Christian books on the shelves, I made short work of them. I had never read so voraciously, simply because the hunger inside me that had been starved to the point of extinction had finally found the sustenance that would satiate it.

In particular, C.S. Lewis's *Mere Christianity* helped me reassess the religion I knew, which was so clouded by empty traditions and rituals as to be almost unrecognizable, and turned it into something tangible, and frankly, likable. It took the bloated institution, filled with flawed people and tainted by the newest novelties and fads, and reduced it down to its most basic, beautiful, life-giving form. Lewis's argument was that humans have an innate moral code built into them that must have been placed there by something:

> We have two bits of evidence about the Somebody. One is the universe He has made. If we used that as our only clue, I think we should have to conclude that He was a great artist (for the universe is a very beautiful place), but also that He is quite merciless and no friend to man (for the universe is a very dangerous and terrifying place).... The other bit of evidence is that Moral Law which He has put in our minds. And this is a better bit of evidence than the other, because it is inside information. You find out more about God from the Moral Law than from the universe in general just as you find out more about a man by listening to his conversation than by looking at a house he has built.[1]

Some of the things he said shocked me, and I remember thinking my pastors and teachers would find them borderline heretical. That, if anything, attracted me to what he was saying even more. He made me realize that Christianity wasn't just a formula or knowing a few facts:

> You can say that Christ died for our sins. You may say that the Father has forgiven us because Christ has done for us what we ought to have done. You may say that we are washed in the blood of the Lamb. You may say that Christ has defeated death. They are all true. If any of them

do not appeal to you, leave it alone and get on with the formula that does. And, whatever you do, do not start quarreling with other people because they use a different formula from yours.[2]

I saw myself in many of his sentences. "When a man is getting better he understands more and more clearly the evil that is still left in him. When a man is getting worse he understands his own badness less and less."[3] His logical and straightforward way to explain everything in the world resonated with me and I felt his was a club I knew I wanted to belong to:

> Give up your self, and you will find your real self. Lose your life and you will save it. Submit to death, death of your ambitions and favorite wishes every day and death of your whole body in the end: submit with every fiber of your being, and you will find eternal life. Keep back nothing. Nothing that you have not given away will ever be really yours. Nothing in you that has not died will ever be raised from the dead. Look for yourself, and you will find in the long run only hatred, loneliness, despair, rage, ruin, and decay. But look for Christ and you will find Him, and with Him everything else thrown in.[4]

When I read this, I felt like Jonah calling out to God from inside the belly of the whale. I prayed, "God, I know my life has ceased to exist, and I'm okay with that. There's not much left to me, but if you want it, you can have it. I am submitting myself completely to you"

I found letting go so liberating, I had to repeat it again and again. I had finally made my peace with God.

The day of my bond hearing finally came. I had been locked up for one week. When I walked in, I saw the new attorney my family had hired for me. I had mixed emotions when I saw my family for the first time since the arrest; my mother, father, Monica, sister Cindy, and brother Kirk. The sight of them made me cry.

I remember the look on my mother's face so vividly. It contained all the sorrow, love, pity, hope, anger, and affection I knew my mother was feeling. I felt so much shame that they were seeing me in prison clothes, wearing handcuffs, and being escorted by two officers. I thought back to a funny little quote from C.S. Lewis that I had just read, which gave me strength. It went, "Now, repentance is no fun at all."

I knew this was a process I had to go through, so I tried to be strong.

The judge realized that I was only a scared kid and that I wouldn't flee the country, so he lowered my bail from $500,000 to $50,000. My family was told they only had to come up with ten percent of this, which they did.

In the afternoon the next day, I was reading in my cell when a silence fell over the entire pod. Someone turned the TV off, and I knew this only happened when a guard entered to announce something. So I waited for and heard the words that every prisoner longs to hear.

"Raymond Cross. Gather your belongings. You're going home."

When I walked out of my cell, I knew I had to do something before I left. I calmly went to every cell and spoke with each inmate I had met during my eight days there. I told them about the peace I had found, and if they wanted the same peace, where they could find it. I didn't do this in a pious, holier-than-thou, evangelistic way. I just felt I had unearthed some hidden secret and I wanted to let them know in case it could help them too. Some snarled and told me where they would like me to go with that stuff, but most were very thankful and appreciated my motives.

I said goodbye to Calvin.

"Don't give nobody your lunch out there, Holly Bally Squally," he said, grinning from ear to ear.

"Okay, Calvin. I promise I won't. You take care of yourself, all right?"

"Yes, sir. Holly bally squally," he said, bowing to me.

After a half hour, the prison guard came in again.

"Raymond Cross! Do you, or do you not, want to go home?"

"Just give me a little more time."

"It's time. Get your stuff."

I slowly packed my stuff. I didn't run out of there like I had thought I would. For some strange reason, I wasn't anxious about getting out of the prison. As far as I was concerned, I had already been released.

## ENDNOTES

1   Lewis, C. S. *Mere Christianity*. New York, NY: HarperCollins, 1952, 29-30

2   Ibid., 156-157.

3   Ibid., 88.

4   Ibid., 190

Above: *Kevin in
December of 1976—
10 years old.*

Right: *Kevin in July,
1984—17 years old*

*The Broward County Sheriff's
Office in Fort Lauderdale.*

*PBA Hall:
The PBA Hall
is where I
hatched the
plan with Paul
to embezzle
from the
Sheriff's Office.*

*The City Limits Club is where I got drunk and told our plan
to the Tomaleri brothers. My slip of the tongue led to the Mafia
finding out.*

## METRO EXTRA

N Sun-Sentinel, Wednesday, February 10, 1988 3B

# Two accused of embezzling over $300,000 from sheriff

**By DAVID UHLER**
Staff Writer

Even though he was barely out of his teens, Raymond Kevin Cross was a talented bookkeeper — so talented that investigators say he was able to embezzle more than $300,000 from Broward County's largest law enforcement agency.

"What he did with the computer, our current bookkeeper still can't figure out," said Cmdr. Judith Meyer, one of his former supervisors at the Sheriff's Office.

An anonymous tip led to the arrest of Cross, 21, of Hollywood, on Friday and the surrender on Monday of his alleged accomplice, ████████ 20, a former savings and loan teller from Pembroke Pines, deputies said.

Each suspect was charged with 127 counts of grand theft, 39 counts of petty theft and one count of organized fraud. Court records show that Cross depos-

ited 166 checks ranging from $10 to $61,000 into two accounts he opened under phony names at Coral Gables Federal Savings and Loan in Miami, where ████ worked.

Investigators said they think Cross and ████ used the embezzled cash for their own high-rolling investment fund.

They may have intended to reimburse the Sheriff's Office account before they were detected, although records say that Cross only was able to sneak $151,000 back in before quitting his job last December.

That left $152,494 unaccounted for, Detective Pete Vazquez said.

"It looks like they were doing it for fun," said Vazquez, an Economic Crime Unit investigator. "We're still checking out the investments, so I can't say anything at all about them."

Through his knowledge of the Sheriff's Office computer, which was replaced with a newer model last month,

Cross was able to erase any traces of the money's comings and goings, Vazquez said.

His manipulation was so masterful it even escaped detection during the annual audit last October at the end of the fiscal year, deputies said.

"We can only hope he made some good investments," sheriff's spokesman Jim Leljedal said. "Then maybe we'll get our money back and then some."

Cross, a Nova University graduate with a bachelor's degree in accounting, started work in May 1986 as the lone bookkeeper at the Sheriff's Office civil division.

While learning the ropes, Cross' interest was apparently drawn to a bank account used for money collected by the Sheriff's Office on behalf of litigants in civil court judgments, Vazquez said.

Investigators said the account holds from $80,000 to $100,000 on any given day. Cross bided his time and waited until January 1987, investigators said.

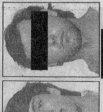

Cross

Then he swung into action, they said. Occasionally using the alias Ira A. Cohen or Raul Cinfuentes, but other times using the names of real litigants for whom money was being held, Cross wrote checks and mixed them in with legitimate bank drafts for authorized signatures, Vazquez said.

Then he hand-delivered them to ████ for deposit at Coral Gables Federal, he said.

Cross and ████ who has worked in construction since quitting his teller's job several months ago, met while attending Florida Christian High School in Hialeah, Vazquez said.

Cross went from full-time to part-time status at the Sheriff's Office last September after starting pre-law classes at St. Thomas University in Dade County. He was replaced after quitting his job in December.

*≈ 17:2*

IN THE CIRCUIT COURT OF THE 17TH JUDICIAL
CIRCUIT    IN AND FOR BROWARD COUNTY, FLORIDA

CASE NO: 80-2356CF A
DIVISION:
ARR.NO: Florida   ROR  IC  CASH  SURETY

STATE OF FLORIDA,          )
          PLAINTIFF,       )
VS.                        )        ORDER OF PROBATION
Raymond K.                 )
Cross    DEFENDANT.        )

THE DEFENDANT, having:        [Counts I - XII Grand Theft 2°
a. X entered a plea of guilty/nolo contendre to:[ XIII - XVIII Grand Theft 1°
b.___been found guilty of:    [
c.___prior probation is hereby revoked:  [

THE COURT HEREBY:
c. X adjudges you guilty of count(s)  III
d. X withholds adjudication of guilt for count(s) 7,9,13,14, & 18

IT IS ORDERED AND ADJUDGED that, subject to the laws of this State:
e. X you are hereby placed on probation for a period of 15 years Ct 3,7,9,13,14,&18
     to be supervised by the Department of Corrections. All other counts work Picsyl Ct concurrent
f.___(split sentence) you shall be confined in:
     1. the custody of the Sheriff of Broward County for a period of ____
     2. the custody of the Department of Corrections for a period of ____
after which you shall be on probation for a period of ____,
to commence upon release.

IT IS FURTHER ORDERED AND ADJUDGED THAT YOU WILL COMPLY WITH, AND CONFORM TO, THE FOLLOWING GENERAL AND SPECIAL
CONDITIONS OF PROBATION:
g.___you must report, in person, immediately or on the next working day after release from confinement, to:
     PROBATION OFFICE, 10 W. Las Olas Boulevard, FORT LAUDERDALE, FLORIDA.
h. X you shall not do any of the following (without first obtaining the consent of your probation officer)
     1. change the place where you live or work;
     2. leave the County where you live;
     3. own, possess or carry on or about your person any firearm or other type of weapon;
     4. associate with any person engaged in any criminal activity;
     5. violate any law of any city, county, state or the United States (a conviction in a court of law is
        not necessary for you to be found in violation);
     6. use any controlled substance, unless permitted by law;
     7. use intoxicants to the extent that your normal faculties are impaired;
     8. visit places where controlled substances are unlawfully sold, dispensed or used.
i. X you must do each of the following:
     1. work diligently at a lawful, gainful occupation;
     2. support yourself and your lawful dependents to the best of your ability;
     3. answer promptly and truthfully any and all questions put to you by either the Court or any probation
        officer;
     4. allow a duly authorized probation officer to visit you in your home, your place of employment or
        elsewhere;
     5. follow carefully and faithfully both the letter and spirit of valid instructions given you by a duly
        authorized probation officer;
     6. file a full and truthful written report with your probation officer, no later than the fifth day of
        each and every month of your probation, upon a form to be furnished you.
     7. pay the sum of $30.00 per month, or any increased amounts authorized by law, for costs of
        supervision while on probation, unless modified as follows: ____

     8. pay the sum of(s) of:
        a) $ waived court costs.
        b) $ waived victim costs on counts ____
        c) $ waived "trust fund" or ____ 50.3 hours community service (F.S.27.3455).
        d) $ waived assessment.
        e) $ ____
        on a schedule to be determined by your probation officer.
        f) $ ____ emergency medical fund.

                    DEFENDANT

*The court's order of probation in Kevin's case.*

*Kevin and his mom during the dawn of Sir Tax—January 1989.*

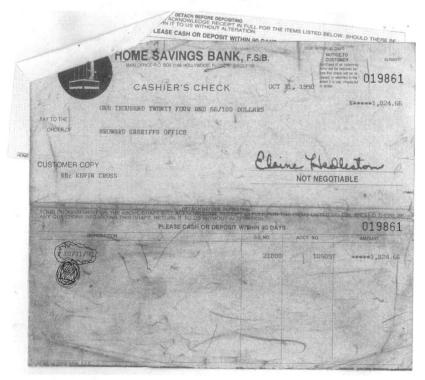

*Kevin was required to make restitution to the Sherriff's Office—a payment toward that debt.*

*Kevin and Stephanie on their wedding day—July 3rd, 1993.*

Today, Kevin speaks around the country in his "Margin and Meaning" seminars.

Kevin and coauthor Steven White

*The Cross family: Kevin, Stephanie, Rachel and Ethan.*

# CHAPTER 9

# losing everything

Monday morning. The day after my arrest.

All of the IBM electric typewriters were humming, spitting out hundreds of subpoenas, summonses, writs of execution, eviction, cease and desist, and writs of this and that. The shock and gossip was in full swing. Behind closed doors, everyone was asking questions, and many were walking by my desk fully expecting something to jump out and self-destruct. A barrier of police tape was created around the perimeter, as if I was holed up inside my desk with a sharp pencil ready to strike.

My dad walked in, dressed in a white, heavily starched shirt, silk tie knotted in a half Windsor, and sporting a tan London Fog trench coat. It was an outfit a middle-aged gentleman would wear when he knew he would soon be let go, or at least subjected to interrogation.

The sudden silence was deafening. Some didn't see him enter the always locked steel door that Melvin had to buzz to unlock. The buzz could be heard in adjacent cities. Most had grown immune to the sound, but today was an exception. At any moment, they all thought, I could walk through the door, grab a cup of coffee, and somehow embezzle thousands of dollars. When they saw my dad, the whispers and gasps erupted.

Without expression, he marched over to the biggest table in the office, which was used for stuffing the obscene amount of envelopes produced by one of the largest sheriff's offices in the country. He threw three newspapers on the massive table and announced to everyone, "This is everything I know." The entire office stared in dead silence as he turned around and walked out.

*The Miami Herald* from that day read:

## SHERIFF'S CLERK CHARGED IN EMBEZZLEMENT
MIKE WILLIAMS Herald Staff Writer

A young bookkeeper with a "brilliant" mind for computers and accounting secretly stole $300,000 from a Broward Sheriff's Office account, then earned $50,000 by investing the money before he was caught, authorities said. Raymond Kevin Cross, 21, who said he blew some of the money on "good times" told investigators he used the money to earn short-term profits and planned to return it before it was missed. He did return $150,000 before he was caught, deputies said.

Cross covered his tracks by erasing sheriff's office computer records of bogus checks he and a bank teller friend deposited in two fictitious accounts at a North Miami Beach bank, investigators said. "This kid is no dummy," said Detective Pete Vazquez. "He's very bright. He had to be to do what he did." The thefts went unnoticed for months until an anonymous caller tipped detectives.

Cross, a 1987 Nova University accounting graduate and St. Thomas University Law School student, was arrested at his Hollywood home Friday. He remained in the Broward County Jail Tuesday, charged with 127 counts of grand theft, 38 counts of petty theft and one count of organized fraud.

The bank teller, Paul Chandler, 20, of Pembroke Pines, was arrested after he turned himself in Monday night. He also faces multiple theft charges. Investigators said Cross, who worked full time in the sheriff's office civil division in 1986 and 1987, stole the money between January and

September of 1987 from an account that handles sums from court judgments.

Cross wrote bogus checks, then hid them in stacks of legitimate checks sent to his superiors for signing, deputies said. He also forged endorsements on legitimate checks, signing the money over to the two bogus accounts, they said.

With Chandler's help, Cross deposited checks totaling $303,494.22 into the two fictitious accounts at Coral Gables Federal Savings and Loan in North Miami Beach, deputies said. Coral Gables Federal officials declined to comment.

Cross's arrest shocked his former superiors, who said co-workers once joked with Cross about his future as a lawyer. "He was very young and appeared to be very bright and intelligent—maybe more than we thought," said Judith Meyer, commander of the civil division.

My father was as shocked as everyone else. He knew suspicions would be high that he was involved, and was sure this meant his job was in jeopardy. It was the hardest time in my dad's career, which grieved me immensely. Everything I did that affected me I was learning to deal with, but what tore at my heart on the inside was the ripple effect it was having on others in my life. When I was stealing, I thought, *Well, at the worst, I'm only paving my own road to destruction.* But in reality, my crime was tearing my family and friends apart as well.

Monica and I had a tearful reunion. On the surface, our relationship appeared to be the same, but something in her eyes had changed. We said the same things as before to each other, but our words seemed empty, as we sat across from each other at our dinner table. Still, she accompanied me to all my subsequent court appearances, which were the only times I saw Paul. He refused to talk to me, or even look in my direction. I think he felt, quite soundly, that my big mouth was the reason we were caught. I sensed shame and regret on his face.

Every time I tried to visit him at his home, I only ended up talking to his mom and his sister, and begging their forgiveness. They gave me it, but I still wanted to tell Paul directly. I couldn't blame him for feeling the way he did, but there were things in me I wanted to say to him. I would sometimes go over the imagined conversation in my head. Often, Paul would forgive me. Sometimes though, I envisioned he would blast me with all the things he would want to say. I never got the opportunity to talk with him.

I never found out who the anonymous caller was that turned me in either, but whoever it was did me the greatest favor of my life.

After I got out of jail, I went into the New Wave Hairstyles salon like usual and started working on the books. A few minutes later, Scott entered and began pacing nervously. Finally, he spoke.

"I dunno, man. You gotta get out of here. I don't need any trouble. I don't want any extra attention here. You got a parole officer? Is he gonna be coming here?"

Before I could answer he blurted out, "Bah, doesn't matter!" Then he began grabbing the books from the desk where I was working. He hurriedly gathered them all in his arms, with papers flying everywhere, and told me I was fired.

The following semester, while waiting for my own day in court, I returned to law school and was welcomed back apprehensively. The other students had a party for me and told me they were hatching a scheme to break me out of jail, so I needn't worry. They were nice guys, but none of them could peg me. They thought I had been a starving student, not knowing I had embezzled hundreds of thousands of dollars. But now I was back and on the straight and narrow, even talking about God and Jesus.

The guys from the law school sent me a big card that said, "Good News Travels Fast." Everyone signed it and added comments like, "Kevin, can I borrow some money?" and "Kevin, can I have some computer lessons?" My professor wrote "I guess I'm in the wrong business."

Needless to say, no one wanted to be my study partner for the rest of the year, so I was on my own. That second semester was trying, but I had a new resolve, and I ended up doing better the second semester than the first.

One day, I was called into the dean's office.

"Mr. Cross, we understand you might be experiencing some legal troubles," the dean began.

"Yes, I guess you could say that," I said, smiling wryly.

"If you get a felony conviction, you will be kicked out of law school. If you don't, you can stay. St. Thomas Law School would like to suggest to you, that if you are going to get a felony conviction, or take a plea bargain which includes a felony conviction, that you ask for a leave of absence before this. If you don't ask for a leave of absence before you get in trouble, we are obligated to show you the door."

"Okay, I think I understand."

"You ask to leave out the back door quietly, or we boot you out of the front," he said more directly.

So I tried not to take a felony conviction, and my attorney did a fantastic job negotiating with the prosecutor from Palm Beach County, Marcia Dugan.

The FBI decided that my crime wasn't racketeering or organized crime. It was just a kid who looked like he knew what he was doing. So they handed jurisdiction over to the state of Florida. This meant Broward County, by default, would handle my trial. The state decided, though, that because my father worked in the Civil Division and my sister worked with the State Attorney's Office, the possibility of bias existed. My case was subsequently handed over to Palm Beach County.

I did some research at the law library of the school, and from what I read, this was a good thing for me. With a federal conviction, you serve your time in a federal penitentiary without hope of a reduced sentence. With a state conviction, you get special considerations based on your behavior, and in all probability, you wouldn't have to serve all your time.

Ms. Dugan asked for a plea bargain that included a request for just one felony count of larceny instead of 300 counts of grand theft. She would withhold my guilty plea for all the other accounts, if I would agree to one count of grand theft felony charge. It sounded like a good deal to me.

The judge said, "Are you sure, Mr. Cross? Keep in mind, if you agree to this, you have in effect just waived all of your rights."

"You honor, I don't care if I don't have any rights. I'm headed for prison if I go to trial."

"You don't know that, son."

"Well, I did some research. That's what they do to people like me. I'm guilty," I said, surprised at my own courage.

I took the plea bargain, and because of that, had to take a leave of absence from law school. My sentence also included ninety days of work release. So, between accepting the plea bargain and turning myself in to the clerk, I had to have a job to be eligible for work release. Since I had just lost my bookkeeping job with Scott at New Wave Hairstyles, I needed to go hunt for a different job.

Under the work release deal, I would work during the day and sleep in the designated pod at night and on the weekends. The work release wasn't as bad as being in jail because most of the guys in there were petty offenders with DUIs, or guys who just refused to pay child support. Surprisingly, these guys complained more than the "lifers" and serious offenders at the jail. They loudly proclaimed how they would prefer to spend their lives in the pod rather than pay their child support. And they were always griping about how the police had treated them unfairly. If you turned a kind ear toward their ludicrous protestations, they would never stop talking about it, so I kept to myself and didn't utter a word of complaint.

After several unsuccessful attempts to find work, I saw an ad in the paper for "Bancor International—Leaders in Travel," a receptive tour operator from Brazil. They wanted an American accountant and were willing to pay $2,000 a month.

When I got to their office to be interviewed, the owners, Gilmar and Jurema Gomes, sat across from me at a shabby desk. Jurema was a frumpy, wrinkled-faced woman whose chiseled hair was dyed about five different shades of blonde. It was as if her hair was desperately fighting against the dye job, charging in waves, and then biting the dust every few inches.

On the desk sat a bag of unshelled sunflower seeds, and every few minutes Jurema would reach into it with her heavily-ringed hand, pull out a handful, and throw them in her mouth. She could position and crunch them so expertly with her tongue, that when she spit them into her hand and placed them on the desk, all that remained was a wet ball of perfectly split shells.

Gilmar, aside from his stringy comb-over and ever-present sneer, maintained a rather youthful look for a man in his fifties. He wore a finely tailored suit and carried himself with an intimidating swagger.

"Elo Mr. Cross, I understand you want to be our comptroller, no?" Jurema said, raising her glasses up to her eyes and looking over my application. I couldn't help but notice her glasses, which were tied around her neck with a giant bejeweled string.

"Yes, ma'am," I said, watching her eyes scan the paper.

"Hmm. What experience do you have, son?" Gilmar asked. The tattered pencil he was chewing distractedly glistened with saliva.

"Well, my degree is in accounting. I worked for the Sheriff of Broward County as an accountant and I was a bookkeeper for New Wave ..."

Before I could finish, Jurema interrupted me by clicking her tongue twice in disapproval. I could see by her face she had seen my conviction on the resume. I knew this was coming.

"What is dis here?" she said, tilting her head and lowering her glasses to scrutinize me disapprovingly. "Ju 'ave a felony? Ju joost came from the jail? Hmm."

I had practiced this speech in my head many times. "Well, yes, I do have a conviction, but those days are behind me," I started. She looked to her husband, who remained expressionless, and then back to me incredulously. I could feel my chances dwindling. "You see, I was just a kid and I ..."

"Espera. Peraí," Gilmar broke in, waving his hand to silence me. He turned to his wife and they started conversing in Portuguese while I sat there, shifting uncomfortably in my chair.

"Ele pode ser útil, querida. Se ele tiver uma condenação, não pode reclamar ou se queixar, sei la."

"Não sei, não sei. E se ele tentar nos roub ..."

"Ele não poder fazer nada! Nada. Nem fazer xixi sem a polícia ficar sabendo. Entendeu?"

A knowing look came over Jurema's face as they appeared to have come to some agreement between themselves. Gilmar reached his sweaty palm across the desk and shook my hand, saying, "Congratulations, you're hired."

My relief was tangible. Every one of my previous interviews had ended abruptly when they discovered I was a felon, so I couldn't contain my enthusiasm at the opportunity.

"Thank you so much," I said, shaking their hands vigorously and grinning stupidly. "You will not regret it, I promise you."

"Hmm. I hope not. Joost be here Monday at 8 o'clock," Jurema said, standing up and ushering me to the door.

I turned myself in to the clerk on June 13, 1988, and started my ninety-day work release program with Bancor. My days and weeks in the work release were desolate and lonely. I spent most of my time laying on my bunk and reading my Bible or praying.

Working for Bancor was a nightmare, but I was grateful to have some work. Jurema would sneak up on me at my cubicle, position her head against my ear, and say loud enough for the entire office to hear, "Kebin! Are ju wuurking?"

I would always turn just in time to see the tiny remains of chewed-up sunflower seeds dotting her tongue.

"Yes, ma'am. I'm working," I would say, sheepishly.

Sometimes they would ask me not to pay the bills. I would protest by arguing that I was in Accounts Payable and should thus pay some accounts, but it fell on deaf ears. Instead, my job became expertly dodging creditors, and stalling until I was given the go-ahead to pay, which was usually several months after the due date.

Gilmar and Jurema would also hold it over my head every day that I was a convicted felon. They were actually doing me a massive favor, and maybe they had a point. They were even generous enough to let me work for free every Saturday to get out of work release. I came to enjoy Saturdays, though, because the office was empty and sometimes my friend Gonçalo da Silva would be there.

Gonçalo was an older Brazilian gentleman. Patient and long-suffering, he would listen intently to my story in great detail as we worked, and would always have a kind word of advice for me. He became an older brother and mentor type to me, often treating me to lunch or inviting me to his apartment to make dinner for me.

The plea bargain I accepted also included fifteen years of probation, which could be reduced if I paid the money back within five years. All told, Paul and I took $300,000 and gave back about half from my investments. The state figured that we owed $125,000, plus the money I had stolen for the down payment on the house. They explained to me that the proceeds from the sale of the house would be handed directly to a representative from the state of Florida. After that, the $125,000 would be divided between Paul and me, leaving us owing $62,500 each. When I added in my credit card debt, I discovered with great dismay that I was more than $100,000 in the hole.

I wondered if the Bible had anything to say about the subject of debt, so I turned to the concordance in the back to look it up. I found two verses. The first was Proverbs 22:7 (NASB): "The rich rules over the poor, and the borrower becomes the lender's slave."

*Yep, I'll be a slave working off that hundred grand.*

Then I turned to the other verse, Romans 13:8: "Let no debt remain outstanding, except the continuing debt to love one another." *God, you must be joking*, I thought. *Surely you must mean every debt except a mortgage or a student loan.* But, the verse seemed pretty clear. I knew I had to get out of debt and stay out.

After twenty-four days of sleeping in the work release bunks, they let me go back home and sleep in my own bed at night. I had to wear a monitor around my ankle that told them where I was at all times. If the phone rang at any time, day or night, I was obligated to run to the phone and plug in my ankle bracelet to tell them I was there.

The weeks and months crept by slowly and painfully, but finally I was released from house arrest. To celebrate, Monica and I went to a nightclub in South Beach called The Strand. I was so elated to be out of the house that I started drinking champagne uncontrollably.

When we left, I grabbed the bottle of champagne that I hadn't finished and tried to take it with me. When the bouncer saw what I was doing, he said, "Hey buddy, you can't bring that with you. What do you think you're doing?"

"Oh, sorry, man," I said, examining the bottle in my hand as if it were some sort of alien machinery. "No problem."

I threw the bottle down on the ground and it shattered, throwing champagne and shards of glass over everyone in the vicinity. I quickly looked up at the bouncer and everyone that was staring at me, and then grabbed Monica's hand and ran. I was too drunk to be embarrassed.

We hopped in the car and sped back home, not even deterred when train barricades appeared before me, blocking the road. I whipped the Saab around the first set, drove along the tracks for a moment, and turned around the second set, gunning the gas as I saw the oncoming train bearing down on us.

When we got back home, I was so nauseous that Monica had to drive me to the emergency room. After arriving, I tried to get out of the car and fell flat on the pavement. They grabbed me and brought me up to an empty room, laid me on the bed, and turned me on my side. I watched, half conscious, as they shoved a tube down my throat and began alternately sending a yellowish liquid into my stomach and sucking brownish-green, viscous fluids out of it. Finally, everything traversing the tube was clear and they gave me the green light to rest.

Monica was visibly sickened by me and began threatening to leave. My relationship with her declined rapidly from that moment on, and there were times when I preferred the jail to my own house. We didn't fight in a traditional, screaming-at-the-top-of-our-lungs sense because I always acted as the peacekeeper, but an icy coldness had crept between us.

I started finding books of matches from bars around town that I knew she was going to. Guys would call at all hours asking for her. My life was hanging from all its hinges. I was convicted of a felony, on probation, working the worst job on the planet, essentially kicked out of law school, my Saab's transmission was shot, and now my wife was undoubtedly seeing other men.

One night, she came to me and said with utter disgust in her voice, "I don't think you'll ever make more than $50,000 a year."

My heart was so wounded. Not only did she feel I was incapable of providing an income, she was really saying to me, "Because I don't think you can bring in that kind of money, I don't want you."

Monica eventually decided to leave me. I felt hurt and rejected, but at the same time I was relieved it was finally over so I could close that chapter of my life. She wanted half the money from the house, but I explained that everything went to paying back the money as I agreed to do. I sold our furniture, and after giving her half the proceeds, she was gone for good.

For a few months, I lived alone in my big, empty house, waiting for it to sell. I don't think I'll ever forget the misery of wearing that ankle monitor, while sitting on the floor (since I had no furniture) and eating ramen noodles nearly every night. Those were horribly lonely times for me. Losing everything I had forced me to examine my disintegrated life, and I didn't like what I saw.

Most jailhouse conversions are just a get-out-of-jail-free card. As soon as you get out of prison, it's "feet, don't fail me now!" as you high-tail it away from God. Although I didn't fall back into my old lifestyle, I wasn't completely back on the straight and narrow. I had given my heart to God, but I wasn't keeping my promise to Him.

To deal with the depression from my situation, I started drinking heavily again. Under house arrest and virtually friendless, I would buy the cheapest booze I could find that would do the trick, and I'd drink alone, yelling internally at myself, God, and anyone who had done me wrong, until I fell asleep.

When my ninety days were up, I shed the ankle monitor and started the humiliating probation process. I had to call my probation officer every day, go to his office once a month, pay the dues, and beg permission every time I wanted to leave the county. I knew my life could not be this way for fifteen years. I had to start paying the money back. I finally sold the house and handed the check directly to the representative from Florida.

Having hit bottom, I had no other choice but to move back in with my parents. My life was reduced to nothing, back to its most basic form, but I was at the beginning of my road to redemption. This was a season of sacrifice for me.

Even after selling the house, I was facing $100,000 in personal debt and still owed the lawyer $25,000 for defending me, so the $2,000 I earned a month from Bancor went directly to paying off the debt. That left me with absolutely zero to buy food or keep the Saab running. In order to survive, I had to get another job.

I had to find something at night, obviously, and a place where I could eat for free. I applied at a few restaurants, but since the shifts all overlapped with my day job, I thought a place like Pizza Hut might be a good option. I could eat as much pizza as I wanted and bring in some extra money to help me get by.

After my Bancor shift, I meandered into the Pizza Hut down the street in Miami and filled out an application. Going from law school and an accounting job at the Sheriff's Office to working at Pizza Hut was a huge blow to my ego, but I had to do what I had to do. At least it was a guaranteed job. If anything, I was overqualified, or so I thought. A few days later I got a call from the manager telling me I was being denied employment. Being turned down was more than I could take.

I knew about one other job possibility. Every day on my way to work, I passed a "help wanted" sign at the Hyatt Regency Miami. It had been there for months, which should have told me something, but I was desperate. They hired me before I even opened my mouth and told me I needed black pants and all-black shoes to work there. I had black pants but not the shoes. The only black shoes on the market were Reeboks that retailed for $50. Spending $50 on shoes was unthinkable to me, so I found an alternative.

McCrory's was a chain "five and dime" store that sold black women's garden shoes with a white stripe around the bottom for $5.99. That was still pricey for me, but I could swing it. I was a size ten, so I went in and bought a pair of size ten women's shoes. At that time, I didn't know that men's and women's shoe sizes are not the same. I was a young kid who hadn't learned important facts like this yet. My toes were doubled over in the shoes, which made my feet look like muffins coming out of the top of them. I had already taken the tags off and put the shoes on, so I couldn't take them back. I certainly didn't have the dough to buy another pair, so I decided to make it work.

When I showed up on my first night of work and greeted my boss, he immediately glanced down at the white stripe on my women's garden shoes. He commented, "Sorry son. They've got to be *all* black. No stripes. Come back tomorrow night with some black shoes."

I was crestfallen. I had literally spent the last of my money on the garden shoes and buying new ones was out of the question. As I was walking back to my car, dejected, I got a great idea—Magic Marker. I remembered having some coins in my car, which I was saving to buy something to eat. I hurriedly gathered them up and bought a black Magic Marker for ninety-nine cents. I returned the next day and started my night job as a valet.

I learned quickly why the "help wanted" sign never left the window of the hotel. The lot where we had to park the cars was about one mile away, so I had to run a mile to pick up cars and another mile back after I parked them. Most tips were about $1 and I could do about twenty cars per shift, which meant a nightly windfall of $20 to eat and buy gas. It was a miraculous feeling to have $20 in my pocket, even when my aching legs could barely walk.

Suddenly the irony of my situation hit me. It wasn't that long ago that I had carelessly blown $1,000 one evening at City Limits. I had promised the valet $50 if he could park my car in the far-away lot and get back in two minutes, as my friends and I were doubled-over, laughing and making fun of him while he scrambled to earn his tip. Then when he didn't make it back in time, I humiliated him by denying him the tip, "Sorry kid. Maybe next time."

Now I was the one scrambling for tips. Maybe God was letting me see life from a new perspective, so I could actually feel what other people go through as they struggle to make ends meet. I would never have chosen to go through this, but I was suffering the consequences of irresponsible behavior. I was like the Prodigal Son, who blew all his money with loose living, and then received an attitude adjustment by going broke and having to feed pigs.

The black stripe on my shoes would continually scuff off as I ran to and from the lot, so I had to pull out the Magic Marker and keep redrawing it between runs. Having to jog in the women's garden shoes made me skip in a decidedly non-masculine way. My running could have been more aptly described as prancing, or maybe even frolicking, something not entirely out of place in Miami Beach in the 1980s.

The income from the valet job was not enough to pay for gas to make it back to my parents' house. I went to the supervisor and bashfully asked him if I could sleep in the lot at night. He agreed, so I started spending every night in the Saab under the I-95 overpass. I lay in the backseat every night with the windows cracked, covered from head to toe with blankets, and hoping that no one would break in and mug me.

This was the same Saab that I had paraded in front of everyone as a testament to my greatness, and now it had become a shameful hiding place. I lay awake at night, sweating and staring into the darkness under the covers, sad and lonely.

How could I have fallen this low? In the span of one year, I had gone from being a young hotshot on my way to a prestigious law school—to homeless and $100,000 in debt. I had lost my job and my house, got arrested, kicked out of law school, and my wife left me. If I had a dog and a pickup truck, it would have been a beautiful country western song.

Life continued this way for months: sleeping in the Saab at night, working all day at Bancor to pay my debt, going directly to the Hyatt Regency at 5:30 P.M., and working until midnight, all just to get money to live.

When my friend Gonçalo heard that I was doing this, he invited me to sleep on the floor at his apartment. Another Brazilian named Ronaldo was already living there and was also sleeping on the floor, so I slept next to him with an old sleeping bag and a pillow. Some nights I would lay awake and stare at the ceiling, thanking God for the pillow under my head and the roof above me. By hitting bottom, I learned to appreciate all those things that I had ignored or despised when I was a rich embezzler.

Ronaldo and I became friends, and he taught me many little ways to stretch money. I had never been on a budget before and didn't know how to get by on nothing. He showed me how to wash my socks with soap every night in the shower, hang them up to dry, and wear them the next day. He taught me how to make countless meals with the most inexpensive ingredients like rice, beans, and bread. Ronaldo and Gonçalo were living with virtually nothing but were always cheerful and content in life, a concept that was puzzling to me. But the more I was around them, the more I was beginning to understand.

One night I was next in line to valet, when a shiny new Jaguar pulled up the ramp and came to a stop in front of me. I was surprised to see Dwight Lauderdale open the driver's side door and jump out. Dwight was a local anchorman, who had done the news on Channel 10 in South Florida for hundreds of years.

*This is my chance*, I thought. *I'll get noticed by a celebrity and he'll see I'm more than a valet. He'll put me on TV, or maybe he can get me a job at Channel 10.*

My mind raced. *What could I say in one sentence or less to impress this guy? Should I make a funny quip, or say something so astute that he will have to pause to think about it?*

He passed me leisurely, and politely nodded.

"Hi, good evening," was all I could muster as I stared psychotically at him. Walking toward the door, he telegraphed a look at me that said, "Does this kid even know how to drive?"

Cursing myself, I hopped into his Jaguar. I looked for the key on the right side of the wheel out of habit, but found that there was no slot. Mr. Lauderdale had stopped at the door and was nervously watching me as I fumbled around his brand new sports car. I finally found the key in a slot located between the seats, and so I grabbed it and turned the key. There was one problem—the car was already on.

The engine let out a blood curdling screech, as I took a year of life out of it. How could I have been so stupid? I popped it into gear, and sped off before Mr. Lauderdale could hunt me down and strangle me. I glanced into the rearview mirror only to see his face contorted in a look of utter horror. If looks could kill, I would not be here today.

Driving to the lot, I changed the radio station (just like they taught me in valet school), and heard a man named Larry Burkett talking about God and money. He was quoting a verse in the Bible I wasn't familiar with. He said, in a calm and soothing voice, "The blessings of the Lord bring wealth and He adds no trouble to it."

The phrase "He adds no trouble to it" shot right into my heart. I knew how to get wealth, but it had always come with a massive dose of trouble and a lot of misery. I couldn't imagine a life that was free from pain and full of blessings. I pulled the car into the lot, and just sat there crying in Dwight Lauderdale's brand new Jaguar.

Larry Burkett kept repeating, "The Earth is the Lord's and everything in it. We are just managers of what He has entrusted us with in this life. Have you been a good and faithful manager with what He has entrusted to you? If not, you need to pray to Him right now and say, 'Lord, I will start to honor you with everything you have given me. I have been a poor manager, but from this moment on, I will be faithful.'"

This had to be the lowest moment in my life. I had hit rock bottom doing it my way. I repeated out loud through my sobs, "Lord, I have been a horrible manager. If you were fair, you'd have fired me a long time ago. I don't have anything right now, but everything I have is yours."

I sat in the car, so transfixed to the radio that I was staring at the dials. The message coming out of the speakers contained the hope I was so desperate to hear. God had tried several times to get my attention. First, when I drove drunk in the wrong direction on the highway, He protected me from getting killed. Then, when the Mafia threatened to kill me, I still didn't get the message. When the FBI and police arrested me and slapped on the handcuffs, it started to wake me up. Finally, when I was assigned a jail cell with a triple murderer, I started reading the Bible. In spite of God's many attempts to get through to me, I still didn't grasp the seriousness of my spiritual condition. Now I was finally "getting it."

"Please take everything I have," I prayed. "I give it all to you, God. You are …"

I was interrupted by a knock at the window by one of the other valets.

"What are you doing, man? You're sitting in there talking to yourself. You okay?" he asked, cupping his hands to the passenger side window and gawking at me.

"Yeah, yeah," I said, nodding my head and motioning with my hands. "I think I'm alright."

I turned my head, and wiped away the tears with my black valet vest. Then, inhaling deeply, I opened the door and ran back to my post with a sublime feeling of weightlessness.

# CHAPTER 10

# love at first sight

The following weeks, I struggled under the heavy hands of the Gomes at Bancor until the day I met Lenny Corsica. Lenny was the maintenance man at the office building. We immediately shared an affinity based on our mutual fear of Gilmar and Jurema.

He and his friend Walter came to get me every day to eat lunch with them. Throwing his brown bag lunch down on the table, Lenny would raise his hands in the air like he was finishing a marathon and start praying earnestly, "Father God, thank you for your blessings of food and shelter and friendship. Oh! How we long now to get away from the world, even from the remembrance of it, and have fellowship with Him that was, and is, and is to come, the Almighty."

"Yes, Lord," Walter exclaimed.

"Lord, we have been worried and wearied, but with you we find rest, all things are with you, and when we live in you, we live in wealth, in constant joy. Lord Jesus, take from us now everything that would interfere with a close communion with you. Remove any wish or desire that might get in the way. What good are idols and other gods? You have seen and observed us. You know our lies and deceptions. Help us be content with what you have given us. We pray this in your divine name. Amen."

"Amen," echoed Walter.

"Now let's dig in, people!" Lenny would say, rubbing his hands together in anticipation. He then proceeded to pull a bologna or ham sandwich out of his bag and devour like it was a filet mignon, pausing after every bite to express his ecstasy with an "mmm" or some sort of elated grunt.

Our lunches together were the only thing that kept me going at Bancor. I sat in wonderment every day at the awe-inspiring voracity with which Lenny attacked life. I was full of discontentment even when I had everything, and this man was praising God for bologna! It made me appraise my lunch, along with everything else in my life, with a new set of eyes. I started uttering little prayers to God, thanking Him for even the most inane things, and my soul would lift and flutter a little every time. I even thanked Him when my mother graciously let me move back into the house that I had so desperately tried to flee.

I started carpooling with another friend from Bancor named Emerson, who hurriedly drove his miniscule Toyota Death Trap through traffic like he was the famous Brazilian race car driver Fittipaldi. Like many Brazilians, Emerson loved Formula One car racing, and it showed whenever his foot hit the pedal. Every morning, I squeezed into the car and gripped my briefcase tightly as he tore in and out of traffic. We would screech to a halt in the closest parking lot in downtown Miami, which was still about a mile from the office, and we'd run the rest of the way in the summer heat.

Gilmar and Jurema waited for us every morning and frowned disapprovingly as we hustled to the door, sweating and panting.

"Hmm, where have ju boys been?" Jurema said. "You know work starts at eight thirty. Ju going to have to work late tonight. Very late. Hmm. Ju are looky I don't call jor probation officer, Kebin. Hmm."

Gilmar chastised us too. "I see you driving, Emerson. Who do you think you are? Fittipaldi? You know, I know Fittipaldi. He is a client here. He comes in here all the time. I know him. The rims on my BMW are from Antonio. You couldn't afford them, Kevin," he said with a laugh.

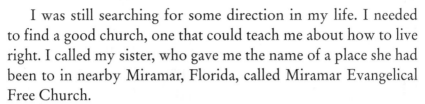

I was still searching for some direction in my life. I needed to find a good church, one that could teach me about how to live right. I called my sister, who gave me the name of a place she had been to in nearby Miramar, Florida, called Miramar Evangelical Free Church.

"I don't want to go to some holy-roller, snake-handling church," I made clear.

"No, no, this is a good church. Trust me. Have you heard of Chuck Swindoll?" she asked.

"I've heard the name, yeah."

"Well, he's a pastor of a big Evangelical Free church. Anyway, just give it a try."

I pulled the Yellow Pages out of my dresser drawer, as I had done almost two years before. Only this time, I wasn't looking for a car mechanic. I was looking for someone to repair *me*. I found a tiny listing for Miramar Evangelical Free Church and dialed the number. The pastor, Dave Evangelista, answered and invited me to come out the next Sunday.

As soon as I walked into the place, I instantly felt at home there. Everyone I met welcomed me enthusiastically, which was so different from walking into bars and clubs where they were only interested in extracting big tips from me. These people were genuinely concerned about me as a human being, with no strings attached.

After the service, I talked at length with the pastor. When I told him about my drinking and asked if he thought it was wrong, he wisely gave me advice that I hadn't considered. He said, "Well, let's look at the big picture. Why would you want to support an industry that ruins lives and marriages? Have you ever thought about how many people have been destroyed by it?" For some reason, it never dawned on me how alcohol had pillaged my life in almost every area.

After I left his office, I was walking down a narrow hallway when I looked up to see someone walking toward me. There she was, bathed in holy florescent light, a woman who looked to me like an angel.

As we approached each other, time slowed to a crawl as I checked her out. She had on a baby blue sundress that made her eyes stand out like two precious stones. Her dirty blond hair fell in descending waves over her cherubic face, and her flawless complexion radiated an innocence too perfect to be expressed by the human tongue. The grace with which she glided down the hall was like wordless poetry to me. I felt as though, even if the hallway was the size of the ocean, I could never make way for her brilliance.

I was jolted back to reality, though, with the thought of all the baggage I was carrying. Monica had moved back to Canada and refused to take my phone calls. Although we were technically still married, I couldn't convince her to sign the divorce papers, so how could I ever go out with a girl like this? I was penniless, married, and a felon on probation who lived with his mother.

I silently prayed, "Lord, if I could ever be with a girl like that … if I could ever have another chance at life …"

I found out her name was Stephanie White. With a name like that, along with her celestial countenance, she took up a residence in my mind that wouldn't leave. Stephanie had come down to South Florida from a Christian college in Indiana. She transferred to a nursing program at Florida International University in South Florida, completely unhitched, and that was enough information for me to spring into action.

I starting showing up at the church for every function I could: singles groups, baptisms, BBQs, Sunday school, church softball leagues, and Bible studies. When I showed up at the weddings of strangers, people would ask, "Who's that guy?" I only attended so I could stand in the back and crane my neck to get a glimpse of Stephanie.

I started going out with the youth group every Sunday night. One night we sat together in Pizza Hut, a place that only reminded me of my inadequacies. I was trying to fit into a group that had no idea where I had been, or about the dangers of the real world. Everyone there was pure and painfully sheltered, which I found somewhat appealing, yet at the same time strangely disconcerting. It made my battered soul looked even more disfigured when dragged into the light with theirs.

They were ordering pizza, drinking soda, and laughing about beach outings, mud volleyball, and what colleges they'd been accepted to. All the while, my mind was drowning in thoughts of Bancor, parole, divorce, and the mountain of debt I was buried under. I was reticent to talk about those things, so I sat quietly, sipping a cup of free water and staring at the pizza, wishing I had the money to buy a slice.

Most Sundays, after the church crowd cleared out, the only ones still hanging around were just Stephanie and me, along with an acquaintance from church named Dave Bosworth. Dave had only two settings: talking and sleeping. Even though he talked a lot, his gregarious nature helped put me at ease in front of the object of my infatuation. My curiosity about her never faltered. I was endlessly enthralled with everything she had to say, and would bombard her with questions about her life, her past, her dreams, and her aspirations. In this way, I avoided revealing my history for a few weeks, but coyness was never my strong suit. I eventually spilled my guts to her late one night in the Pizza Hut parking lot.

She sat and listened non-judgmentally to my every word, nodding with such a look of care on her face that I couldn't help but open up and confess every sordid detail. I knew the kind of woman I wanted: someone without guile, not jaded or money-hungry, and free from pretense or duplicity. Steph was the personification of all these things, a pure, heaven-sent gift.

Now came the hard part. How could I win her over and persuade her parents that I wasn't a bum? How could I convince them that I had fixed my life and wouldn't ruin hers?

I knew I needed to finalize things with Monica, so I filed the uncontested divorce papers myself. She never responded, so I initiated a procedure called "Constructive Service of Process." I had to advertise in *The Miami Herald*, a paper with a circulation of about 400,000, which said that I, Raymond Kevin Cross, was seeking a divorce. The ad had to detail my attempts to reach her and run for ninety days before the judge would sign the uncontested divorce.

Even though I was ashamed and desperately trying to hide my past, I was forced to broadcast my monumental failings to the world. After ninety days, Monica still had not responded and I was granted the divorce. I was now free to dream of Stephanie. I only heard from Monica once after that, several years later, when she called trying to collect on a watch she had given my sister.

I asked Stephanie out and she agreed, on one condition. I would have to ask her parents first. *No sweat*, I thought. The next week, I was summoned to meet her folks and formally state my intentions with their first-born daughter.

The days leading up to the dinner with her parents, Tom and Cheryl, were spent going over all the possible scenarios in my head, belaboring every detail in my mind. What should I wear? How should I act? What kinds of questions are they going to ask me? What if they want to know about my past?

I paced back and forth in Gonçalo's little apartment, nervously practicing everything I would say to Mr. and Mrs. White. One moment I was envisioning everyone around the table laughing jovially at my well-placed jokes, and the next I was seeing myself running from the house, kicking up a cloud of dust in my wake.

I imagined entire conversations in my mind and played the part of Stephanie's parents: "Why, Kevin, you are the finest young man our Stephanie has ever met. We would be honored if you would date her. Please pass the zucchini."

Finally, the fateful day arrived. I donned my best clothes and drove to the house, practicing my lines out loud the entire way. When I got there, I rang the doorbell with a sweaty finger and took a deep breath.

The door swung open to reveal Stephanie's mom, Cheryl, a woman in her forties with short, black curly hair. Behind her was Stephanie's eight-year-old brother, Steven, who was peering at me like a kid stares at a monkey his first time at the zoo. Apparently, there had been enough discussion prior to my arrival to pique his interest. Maybe he knew something I didn't.

"You must be Kevin," Cheryl chirped as she shook my hand. "Come on in. Dinner's on the table already. Steven, wash your hands!"

At this, Steven darted off and Cheryl led me to the dining room where Stephanie's dad was already seated at the head of the table.

"Kevin, this is Tom, Stephanie's father," Cheryl said, heading to the kitchen to attend to the meal.

My face must have been flushed and beet-red with nerves, because all of the sudden, alone with Tom, I felt hot and a little dizzy. Somehow I reached my hand out to him and managed to say, "I'm Kevin, how do you do, Mr. White?"

He regarded me with a patriarchal air, arose from his chair, took my hand tightly, and shook it deliberately. "I'm fine. Call me Tom. You find the place alright?"

"Oh, yes sir, no problem at all." I couldn't remember any of the lines I had practiced, so I stood there for a few seconds, looking around the room and racking my brain for something to say. Luckily, Cheryl walked in at that moment carrying a casserole dish, followed by Steph's sister Carmen, little Steven, and finally Stephanie herself.

"Okay, let's eat!" Tom said, slapping me on the back and motioning to the chair next to him. "You're right here next to me."

Tom prayed and everyone started eating except me. My nerves were shot and food was the last thing on my mind.

"Don't you like our food?" Tom asked with a calculating grin on his face.

"Yes sir. I, I love the food. It's fantastic."

"In this family, the rule is, as long as you've got one foot on the ground, everything is fair game. You're not being rude unless you pick both feet up, so dig in," Cheryl said helpfully, noticing my reluctance.

I was there to fit in, so I lifted out of my chair, one foot still on the ground, and grabbed the dish of mashed potatoes across from me, accidentally knocking the gravy boat over and spilling gravy over the fresh table cloth. I grabbed it immediately, apologizing to anyone who would listen. I had wanted to make a good first impression, but wasn't starting out too well.

"It's fine. Don't worry about it, Kevin. The tablecloth never makes it through a whole meal intact. Besides, there's more where that came from," Cheryl said, grabbing the boat and running to the kitchen with it.

"So, Kevin, what'd you come here for tonight?" Tom asked, taking a bite of chicken.

"Well, I want to ask to date your daughter." I was sweating almost visibly now.

"Uh-huh. Well, let me ask you this first. Where do you see yourself in twenty years?"

I could see by his face that he was enjoying this too much. I think he half-intended me to find this humorous as well, but I couldn't muster a laugh and just gave a sickly smile.

It was a question I hadn't foreseen. All I could think about was getting out of debt, finishing my parole, and marrying Stephanie, but I thought I had better not mention that. I was searching for something wise to say, but it would look bad if I took too long to think about it, so I blurted, for no apparent reason, "Santa Monica."

As soon as I said it, I recognized its stupidity and finally let out a small laugh. He remained stoic, nodding his head as if I had said something worth contemplating.

"So, Kevin, tell us what you do," Cheryl asked.

Finally, a question I could answer.

"Well, I am a comptroller for a travel company called Bancor. They handle Brazilian tourists here in South Florida. My dream, though, is to start a business."

"What kind of business are you thinking of getting into?" Tom asked.

"I do taxes. That's what my degree is in, accounting. From Nova. Nova Southeastern."

"I see. So, why should I let you date my daughter?" he persisted.

I couldn't blame him. It's a father's job to protect his daughter from would-be scoundrels, but I didn't know you were supposed to relish it so much.

"Tom, let the poor boy eat!" Cheryl exclaimed, coming back from the kitchen and setting the fresh gravy in front of me.

"Yeah, Dad," Carmen echoed.

I quickly cast a furtive glance at my new allies, looking for help wherever I could find it. I even peeked down at little Steven, hoping maybe he could offer some solace, but he was gobbling down his chicken, completely unaware of my pain. I thought Stephanie might jump to my aid, but she was staring down at her plate, chewing daintily and avoiding any eye contact with me.

"Well, sir, I am working on being a godly man," I stammered. "I mean, I just gave my life over to God and I want to treat your daughter like a woman, a godly woman, that is. God got a hold of my heart. You know what I mean?"

Instead of answering, he plowed on. "I, we, have heard some interesting things about you. How do we know you don't want to take advantage of our daughter?"

"Well, uh, I don't," I stammered, thoroughly beaten. "Your daughter is an incredible girl, um, a pure woman and I, uh, just want to treat her, like I said, like a godly woman."

The entire night continued like this, fielding a barrage of questions, making attempts at small talk, and laughing nervously when I thought it was appropriate. I felt like a boxer who'd been pummeled; barely conscious and just trying to protect my face. I don't know who was answering these questions, but it wasn't me.

Finally, my misery abated and I bade farewell. On the drive home, I thought, *I answered all the questions asked of me tonight like a champ. They should give guys some sort of manual for these situations. Maybe I'll write one.*

Stephanie called as soon as I got home with the verdict. She informed me her parents had decided that for now, I would be able to see her only at home in a family environment. At first I protested, but then I remembered I could see her at church, youth group, and though it was uncomfortable, once a week at her house. I could live with that.

I lay awake all night in my sleeping bag on the floor, grinning and dreaming about my sweet future with Stephanie.

# CHAPTER 11

# starting the firm

Word spread around the office that I did tax returns. One by one, everyone approached me to do their taxes, and soon they were recommending me to their brothers, parents, and cousins. Getting paid $75 to $100 per return was huge money for me, and I started building up a small client base.

One particularly miserable day, I was sitting at my desk staring at the Sir Speedy calendar that hung in my cubicle, when suddenly I hit upon an idea. I decided to leave Bancor after a year and a half of indentured servitude, and I would become "Sir Tax," freelance accountant extraordinaire.

I immediately called the number on the Sir Speedy calendar and had my own business cards printed. I hung up the phone, walked to the Gomes's office, and triumphantly handed in my two weeks notice to Gilmar and Jurema.

At the end of the two weeks, I stopped by their office to say goodbye.

"Goodbye, Kebin. Ju want to resign? So, don't expect a check for de last two weeks. We are not going to pay ju! Now get out of here," Jurema said, trying with little effort to suppress her displeasure.

I walked out feeling unappreciated for the work I had done for them, but determined to make it as Sir Tax. I went to a place called the Shawny Hotel that I had worked with through Bancor, and got a part-time job to help get my new business off the ground. When I showed up for work the first day, I walked into the lobby to see my manager whispering with an all too familiar face, Gilmar Gomes. I froze and pretended to tie my shoe until Gilmar left, at which point the manager walked over to me and calmly said, "Sorry, Kevin. It's just not going to work out with us."

I didn't even wait for an explanation, knowing that Gilmar was so upset about my leaving Bancor that he had smeared my name with the manager to pay me back. I later looked back on this and realized he had done me a favor because it pushed me in a better direction. I just turned on my heels and walked out the door, wrestling with the tie I had just bought for the job.

*Okay, if I can't get a job,* I told myself, *I will get out there and pound the pavement.*

With business cards in hand and my shirt neatly pressed the way Ronaldo had taught me, I set out on foot to call on every business in the area. The first week of canvassing, every single person turned me down flat, except for one individual. Rose, who owned Rose's Beauty Salon said, "You know what, hon," she said sweetly, "I'm going to hang on to this card. I've got some friend who might want to call you."

Since I couldn't afford to rent my own space, I set up a pitiful little office in the back room of my mother's house. From the living room I borrowed a ratty old desk and a wooden chair that creaked and groaned, even with the smallest of moves. My mother loaned me $1,000 to buy a computer and a printer, and Sir Tax was born.

Borrowing the money made the acids eat away at my stomach, so I worked feverishly to pay her back as fast as I could. That was the last money I ever borrowed. I hung Psalms 127:1 (NASB) on the wall which read, "Unless the Lord builds the house, they labor in vain who build it." This Scripture became a constant reminder for me to live right.

Every morning I got up early so I could get to Miami's metro system during rush hour and hand out business cards to everyone on the train. I did everything I knew to do to get my name out there. Although I wasn't soliciting business at my church, it wasn't long before several members approached me to do their taxes.

My Sir Tax office was finally starting to come alive. The desolate sounds of a lone keyboard and a creaking chair were a symphony to my ears, as I plodded along alone in the back room of my mother's house. I thought, *Even if I make $100 a month, this is much better than working under the thumb of Bancor.*

Business started to pick up via word of mouth, and soon I had more clients than I knew what to do with. It got so hectic that there were nights when I had clients arriving at midnight, their headlights illuminating the entire office for a split second as they pulled into the lone grass parking space in the back yard.

I had heard the old saying a million times that "money can't make you happy," and I certainly found that out when I was stealing. But now, since I was earning it legitimately, I figured it would bring me at least some sort of contentment, or maybe even happiness. I set my goals to disprove the adage, following the worldly wisdom of writer Spike Milligan who said, "All I ask is a chance to prove that money can't make me happy."

This became my new path. Since stealing it hadn't worked out, I would work day and night to fill my coffers legally, buy a nice car and a big house, and live the American dream with 2.5 kiddies and Fido. My new god was just being born, opening his eyes, stretching his arms, and emerging from the womb with a big grin on his face.

I kept my word with Steph's parents, only seeing her at church functions and family dinners. Because I showed up for dinner two or three times a week, I was beginning to ingratiate myself. I raved about the meals, washed the dishes after dinner, played "Teenage

Mutant Ninja Turtles" with Steven, and respectfully agreed with anything asked of me. They were a God-fearing family, and I was starting to actually enjoy their company and look forward to my evenings there.

Finally, after more than eight months, her family relented and agreed to let me go on a date with her on October 13, 1990. I was so shocked that I didn't know what to do. I had not prepared for the day I would actually be alone with her.

For our first date, I decided to make dinner for the two of us in the backyard of my mother's house. I set up a beach scene using a small table with two chairs and a candle. I wanted some tunes, so I ran into my office, grabbing the stereo and the tapes that I deemed to be the most romantic. I had intended to put on a black suit for the occasion, but decided to make dinner first in case I spilled something.

As I was making a linguini pasta with shrimp, I heard the doorbell ring.

*Steph is here early! I can't let her see me like this,* I frantically said to myself. I was wearing old, torn-up khaki shorts with a gaping hole in them which I had stapled shut, and a paint-stained T-shirt with sweat marks under the arms. I didn't have time to change clothes, so I opened the door, shielding myself with it, and stuck my head around it to make sure it was her.

As I expected, Steph was standing in the doorway. She looked so soft and demure in the fading sunlight, and her perfume made my heart melt.

"Wow. You look so, so amazing. Would you excuse me real fast? Go check out the backyard," I said, pointing out the direction. "I'll be right back."

Quickly I changed clothes, putting on my one good suit, and then, playing the role of chief chef and headwaiter, I served her my home-cooked dinner. Although we were both shy and soft-spoken, we felt so comfortable with each other just to be ourselves. *This is what I've been missing,* I thought.

We started dating as much as her parents would tolerate, which wasn't as often as I would have preferred. On our shared birthday, November 19, I took her to John U. Lloyd State Park, where we strolled on a little wooden walkway shaded by giant banyan trees. As we were walking, hand in hand, I was suddenly filled with a moment of courage.

I pulled her to me, leaned in, and kissed her passionately. We had known each other for nine months and it took that long for me to work up the nerve. The feeling of this angel's gentle lips against mine was like a blind man finding sight, or a man lost in the desert finding a cool, clean stream.

Even though I was ashamed of an impure past, this relationship was entirely different from anything I had known. It was like I had a totally clean start, that I was a young man in high school again, and this was the very first kiss I had ever had.

That night when I went to bed, I felt like I was floating on cloud nine.

After working six months out of the back room, I had paid my mother back everything that I had borrowed from her. It became clear that I would need to rent an office somewhere, so I found a place on Young Circle in downtown Hollywood. I shared the office with a Christian lawyer, and soon my business was flourishing. I even scraped up enough to run an advertisement on TV. The commercial featured a grainy video of me with stars floating by in the background, and a jingle written by my sister on an acoustic guitar:

*Sir Tax Services are number one,*
*The affordable tax experts that get the job done.*
*After working hard all year you don't have to fear,*
*Cause Sir Tax Services will end your year with cheer!*

The only spot I could afford was late at night, so it ran at 2 A.M. with little fanfare, but it gave the business a nice kick-start.

All my income had gone to paying off the debt to my mother, so with that out of the way I could now start accumulating for myself. The allure of the world was still calling me. This first taste of success was like a cool breeze to Ramone Simone, who had lain dormant for almost a year. Although I didn't call him by that name anymore, he was stirring around inside me again.

I leased another Saab, this time a black one, and justified it by telling myself, *God wants me to have it. There's nothing wrong with driving a nice car and having nice things as long as you're doing the right thing. I have to drive a successful car to show people I'm successful. It's just a sleek, chrome-encrusted blessing from Him for living right. God wants me to show others the blessings that can be theirs if they follow Him. Who's going to sign up to be a Christian if they see I'm poor and destitute?*

My conversion was a slow one. It was a "peace" by "piece." Every time I would get right with the Lord in one area of my life, another area would crumble. I would rush to cover the broken place, and as soon as I felt good again, some other part of my life would collapse.

Although I had given my heart to God in every other area of my life, my finances remained mine. I stopped cursing, using drugs, and drinking. I went to church every Sunday and did charitable works, but I still felt I had to keep up a certain lifestyle.

My Christian partner had also leased a sports car and we were determined to make a ton of money the "right" way. As the weeks and months flew by, I started to suspect something was wrong. My partner was acting suspicious, and I caught wind that he was planning to take some things from the office while I wasn't there. I decided to start sleeping at the office, jealously protecting the few possessions I had accumulated since being jailed.

One night I called my sister, who still worked for the police department, and she came to the office to wait with me. We changed the code on the alarm system, and sure enough, around three o'clock in the morning, my partner pulled up in a van with his father and another helper. They stealthily went to the door and punched in the old code, igniting the alarm and sending them running. They had planned to steal all the office furniture and sell it.

After he moved out, I was stuck with the rent for the rest of the contract. As soon as it was up, I moved to a small commercial office on the same street for $325 a month. It was about the same size as my mother's back room, but it needed some remodeling.

I recruited my entire family to help fix it up, and we made it into a nice boutique-style office. I still didn't have any credentials as an accountant because I was a convicted felon, and I couldn't legally take the test to become a CPA for several more years. I finally gained admittance into something called the NATP, the National Association of Tax Practitioners.

*I'm finally somebody*, I thought.

Around the same time, I looked into Larry Burkett's organization, Crown Financial Ministries. He was responsible for helping turn my life around, and I wanted to be that guy for other people who may be going down the same road I had already traveled. I decided to attend their training to become a seminar instructor and Biblical financial counselor.

A few weekends a month, I had the opportunity to speak to hundreds of people, telling them my story, and warning them about the consequences of misusing money. My practice also became a free financial counseling clinic for those who were struggling with their finances.

One day a guy who was running for public office came by and asked for my help. He was a school principal and his wife was a teacher, and they were being audited for deducting teacher-related expenses. I was so eager to help that I accepted the job on the spot, and agreed to represent him in front of the IRS.

To prepare myself to represent them, I studied the one little accounting publication I had for about a week. When the day finally arrived, I put on my best suit and acted like I had done this sort of thing a thousand times. We all sat down at a big conference table: the principal, a supervisor, an auditor from the IRS, and me.

The first thing they asked me was, "Mr. Cross, are you an EA, CPA, or J.D.?"

I panicked. I wasn't even sure what that last one was. I stammered, "Uh, um, I'm a, uh, member of the NATP."

They stared at me blankly for a moment and asked, "What's that?"

I swallowed hard. "That's the National Association of Tax Professionals."

They looked at each other with raised eyebrows, barely suppressing a laugh, and said, "Look, you have to have these credentials to represent somebody. So, you can sit here and we'll talk to them, okay?"

I shrank back into my chair, all the blood rushing to my face at once. As they talked for another hour, I shifted uncomfortably in my chair, wondering how much longer I would be tortured. When they were done, the principal gave me a ride home.

I didn't know what to say except that I was sorry, which I repeated the whole way home. He finally said, in the way a father would talk to a kid who just lost a Little League baseball game, "Do you want to stop for a sub?" I really just wanted to get home and hide as soon as I could, but I feebly accepted and choked the sub down in complete silence.

When I got back, I felt like a whipped pup. I started researching what all those things meant. I knew I couldn't become a CPA yet, and a J.D. was for somebody who went to law school, so those were out. I decided I would have to become an EA, an Enrolled Agent. I studied for months and finally passed the exam, only to find out that I couldn't actually practice as an EA until the five years were up on my probation.

Unfortunately, or maybe fortunately, the parole officer assigned to me was a sadistic woman in her fifties who loved to treat me like a lowlife. I constantly had to call and check in with her, and whenever I wanted to leave the county, I had to go to her begging.

One day my sister, who lived outside of South Florida, called me in a panic, asking if I could come up to watch her kids. She and her husband were leaving that day for the weekend, and their babysitter had fallen through. I told her I would, and immediately called my parole officer. She didn't pick up, so I tried several more times to no avail. Finally, I left a message with her explaining what was happening, where I would be, and how to contact me.

When I returned on Monday, I called to tell her I was back. She told me that since I had not gotten permission from her, she was going to violate me. That meant I would have to spend the rest of my sentence, four years, in prison.

I was stunned, not to mention terrified. *Four years in prison?* How could she do such a thing to me when I clearly explained the situation? I had seen bigger hearts in an artichoke than what she had.

My insides were in turmoil the entire time I was waiting to explain my side of the story to the judge. Finally, I appeared before Judge Fleet, a stern, elderly man who scowled down at me from the bench.

"Son, how much community service do you do?" he shouted down at me.

"Well, I do quite a bit," I muttered sheepishly.

"How much are you supposed to do?" he yelled, even louder this time.

"Your honor, it wasn't part of my agreement to do any community service, but ..."

"Well, now," he scoffed, "you're going to do fifteen hours a week! How does that sound to you?"

"Yes sir, your honor." Although I didn't want to show it, I was relieved and thankful for his sentence. What's fifteen hours of community service compared to four years in prison? I started volunteering at a local food shelter for fifteen hours a week, which ended up being the most gratifying times of my life. They were also the hardest.

Stephanie and I had been dating seriously for more than a year, and we had talked about getting married. I was keeping my promise to her by paying off all my debts to the state before we tied the knot, so we could get started without financial obligations. My dream of having a life with her, and a house full of little kids running around looking half like her and half like me, was all too real. And then, it happened.

Steph decided to go on a missions trip to Ecuador for a month during her summer break. I was fine with that. But when she returned, she gave me the crushing news that she had met someone there. She had met Dave, a missionary pilot who worked with the indigenous people of Ecuador. They hit it off big time, and Stephanie told me we could no longer see each other. She was sure she wanted to be with a missionary, someone nobly dedicated to doing God's work.

I was devastated. If you've ever had your heart broken, pulled out of your chest, and stepped on, you know exactly how I felt, except multiply your pain by ten times.

She told me her parents were encouraging her to not be hasty and to explore her options. Dave had planned to come to South Florida on furlough, so they encouraged her to see if the connection that had blossomed was real.

My heart was absolutely shattered. Stephanie was the love of my life, and I thought I was building a close relationship with her family, even acting as a counselor of sorts when they had problems. I had spent eight months at their house, just trying to prove to them that I could be trusted to go on a date with her, and so it tormented me that they would even entertain the thought of their daughter being with someone else.

Dave came up from Ecuador and spent one fun-filled week with Stephanie, which was one agonizing week for me. They were inseparable, going on dates and spending time with her family. He accompanied her to her graduation from nursing school, which I had imagined myself doing.

I was sick. My thoughts were consumed, day and night, with what they were doing. I imagined the worse as I lay in my single bed at night. I was standing by helplessly, as my true love was falling in love with someone else. I felt like the old, familiar dog in a family that had just gotten a cute new puppy.

My abject misery finally abated when Dave returned to Ecuador with nothing decided. With him out of the picture, I went to work romancing Stephanie again, hoping to win her heart back.

At first, her mind would wander back to Dave in Ecuador. Still, I knew that my presence with her was more tangible than her thoughts of him. I treated her like a queen, trying to show her I was the guy for her, not him. I knew that she wanted to be a missionary, so I did my best to convince her that I was a missionary, too. I was going to be a "financial missionary." My mission in life was to set people free from debt and help them use their money to further God's kingdom. She liked that idea and could see the need for that ministry.

After several months of wooing, her feelings started coming back to me, and to my relief, we formed a relationship like we had before. She actually fell in love with me again, and we started talking again about our plans to get married and how we could carry out our mission.

I had nearly been mortally wounded, but it turned out to be an incredible, faith-stretching exercise for me. Forgiving, and especially forgetting, are acts that take immense effort. Forgiveness seems to go against our very nature, but when done with a pure heart, offers a transcendent glimpse of the divine we would otherwise miss.

After dating Steph for almost four years, I made the final payment to the Sheriff's Office and the credit card company. For the first time in what seemed like an eternity, I was now debt-free. I then went in front of the courts and was relieved to hear that my parole had been finally lifted. The great burden I had carried for four years was gone, and I could breathe as an unfettered man.

I now realized that even when I earned my money legitimately, I couldn't worship the money god, or try to impress others with my wealth. I joyfully ditched the Saab and bought a "bare bones" white Saturn full of character that was ten times the car the Saab was. I had fulfilled my promise to Stephanie, to the state, and most importantly, I had followed God's instructions: "Let no debt remain outstanding, except the continuing debt to love one another, for he who loves his fellow man has fulfilled the law" (Romans 13:8).

Stephanie and I were married a month later in a little ceremony at Miramar Evangelical Free Church. We moved into a tiny, one bedroom apartment for $450 a month, which gave us the opportunity to save our extra money. By taking all of our extra wedding presents back for a refund, we were able to put $2,500 into a house fund. We lived simply and frugally according to God's plan.

I learned that God's Word not only contains the secret to real happiness, it also has a practical financial blueprint for success. We decided to live on a spending plan, avoid debt like the plague, save regularly, and live below our means. We carefully honored God with our money and possessions, and followed His financial plan to the best of our ability. As we saved all of Steph's nursing income, I continued the fledgling tax practice, finally receiving my EA license in 1994, which qualified me to represent clients before the IRS.

By living on a tight budget, we were able to buy our own house just a couple years later. We made a down payment of $77,000, which was half the price, and paid off the mortgage in just four years by following the principles in God's Word. It wasn't because the business was bringing in a lot of money. It wasn't. We had set our minds to paying it off and followed God's simple plan of frugality and faithfulness.

The business continued to grow and soon I was in need of my own building. On a whim, I went into an old run-down real estate office on one of the busiest roads in South Florida. Inside, the place was a mess; files were stacked haphazardly on the floor, the walls were made of faux wood paneling, and the carpet was ripped and stained.

After I entered, I heard someone faintly say, "Back here."

I followed the voice through a maze of filing cabinets and mountains of stray papers, and saw a small, balding guy sitting behind an aging desk.

"Hi there," I said, choking on the dust. "I'm your neighbor down the street, and I just wanted to let you know that if you ever want to sell the place, I'd be interested."

"You know what? I wanna retire. Make me an offer."

Looking around at the dilapidated walls, I decided to shoot low.

"Well, how about $100,000?" What was I doing? Did I just make an offer on this place?

"How 'bout $300,000?"

*I know this is commercial property, but that's seems expensive,* I thought. "How about $200,000?"

"$235,000. And I'll finance it for you."

"I'll have to think about it," I said, in total shock.

I left and spent the next couple weeks praying and talking to my wife about it. I was still renting an office and had to find a way out of it, if I was going to take the deal. I was tempted to not say anything and just move out, but I knew God would not honor those actions. I resolved to go to my landlord, who was a Christian, and tell him the situation.

When I spoke to him, he just wanted to know the deal. He told me he was so glad I had come to him, and he graciously decided to let me out of the contract early. He did something godly that didn't make sense from a business perspective, but was greatly appreciated by someone needing a break.

I couldn't convince the seller to go down on the price, but I got him to agree to come down on the interest rate from 8¾ to 8% percent. What he didn't realize was that by lowering the interest, I had just shaved $10,000 off the price.

The only reason I was able to consider buying my own office was because I had paid off my house and was completely debt-free. Nothing was holding me back, so when the opportunity arose, I had the freedom to take it. I used the same method as the house, living frugally, and putting all my profits into paying the building off. And again, after just four years, it was completely mine. We renovated everything and turned the office into the leading Christian tax practice in South Florida.

Around the same time, I passed the CPA exam and received my Masters in Taxation from Florida International University, which made me finally feel like a legitimate accountant. God sent clients, sometimes from the most unlikely places at the most opportune moments, to bless the business and make it successful.

When we brought our precious children, Rachel and Ethan, into this world, we were debt-free, had our own house, a burgeoning tax business, and a godly marriage. God had honored His already-lopsided agreement with me: If I will honor Him with everything I have and do, in return I will get to keep this incredible joy that dwarfs anything the world ever offered me.

And He wasn't done with me yet.

# CHAPTER 12

# from criminal to financial counselor

E very Thursday, the Sir Tax office would close so that we could offer free financial counseling to anyone who had a need. The overwhelming satisfaction I got from helping others made the drudge of the rest of the week worth it. I saw many cases of heartache, in much worse situations than my own, and was able to tell them exactly what to do because I had gained insights from my own experiences.

Over the years, it was exciting to see so many desperate people come through my doors, turn their lives over to God, and then get out of the messes they were in. Watching God come through on His promises every single time was a source of constant, life-giving pleasure for me. But sometimes it took awhile for these clients to figure out the real problem.

"Get Rich Maria" was a single mother who came to me one Thursday, harried and in a hurry. I called her that because her mail address was getrichmaria@somethingorother.com. She flew into the office, pulled up a chair, and brushing the bushy brown hair from her eyes, proceeded to tell me her story.

"So," she said, exhaling loudly, "I am a single mother with a handicapped child and I *know* God wants to make me rich."

"Okay," I said, "you need financial counseling?"

"Yes, I do. Because I'm really deep in debt," she uttered with an edge in her voice, reaching into her purse and pulling out one by one what appeared to be overdue bills.

"It's okay. We will go over your bills later. Right now just tell me what you are doing about it."

"I'm working three jobs right now, but Kevin, I have been praying for a new BMW. I know God is going to bring me a BMW," she said, completely serious.

I reached for the Bible, turned to James 4 and started reading:

*You want something but don't get it. You kill and covet, but you cannot have what you want. You quarrel and fight. You do not have, because you do not ask God. When you ask, you do not receive, because* you ask with wrong motives, that you may spend what you get on your pleasures. (James 4:2-3, NIV)

I read the last line with emphasis, and then looked up to see a look of shock and offense on Maria's face.

We reluctantly struggled through the rest of the session, Maria eying me warily for fear I may tell her something even more offensive.

After a month had passed, Maria stopped by the office again for her next session, full of vigor.

"Kevin! You won't believe what happened. You'll never believe it. It's a miracle," she said with a look of glee in her eyes. "I just totaled my car!"

"Oh, no. That's tragic. Is everyone okay?"

"No, no, no. You don't understand. Now I know God wants me to have a BMW."

"Okay, tell me a little more about that," I said, not believing my ears.

"Okay, I know the one I want already. It's this two-seater convertible BMW ..."

"But you have children, don't you?"

"Yeah."

"One who's handicapped right? Who needs to be in a wheelchair in the back?"

"Yeah," she replied indignantly.

"The two-seater isn't going to have room for him ..."

"But I still know God wants me to have it."

Once again, I pulled out the Bible. This time I turned to Luke 11:1-3 and read aloud:

> *One day Jesus was praying in a certain place. When He finished, one of His disciples said to Him, "Lord, teach us to pray, just as John taught his disciples." He said to them, "When you pray, say: Father, hallowed be your name, your kingdom come. Give us each day our daily bread."*

I stopped there.

"Maria, you need bread, don't you?"

"Yes."

"You need to ask for daily bread. You're asking for a BMW. He wants to give you bread. You're asking for a Mercedes. He wants to give you mercy. Do you see the difference in this prayer and the prayer you are praying?"

I could see her thinking of a comeback, but something was stopping her.

"Maria," I said, taking her hand, "Do me a favor. Close your eyes and think. What is the most important thing in your life?"

She obliged and shut her eyes tightly. Several long seconds passed silently, and then I saw her lip begin to quiver and a tear formed on her clenched eyelids. First one tear fell, then her whole face welled up and soon she was sobbing.

"My children. My ... two ... boys," she choked.

Making a single mother cry might be one of the worst offenses in the world, but I pushed on.

"The three, four jobs you're working right now, you're not even seeing them," I said, handing her several tissues. "And you are thinking that getting a BMW is going to satisfy you, but it won't. It just won't. Can you close your eyes for me again? I want to read something to you. This is from Matthew11:28-29: 'Come to me, all you who are weary and burdened, and I will give you rest. Take my yoke upon you and learn from me, for I am gentle and humble in heart, and you will find rest for your souls.' Maria, your yoke is so heavy. When are you going to start asking for bread instead of a BMW?"

For one of the first times in my life, I saw someone break. Her petite frame gave way and shook, as the tears rolled wildly down her face, smearing her makeup and wetting her blouse. It was as if the crippling burden she had been carrying had been lifted all at once.

I thought, *Oh, thank you God for letting me witness this. Thank you for letting me be a part of this.* Little did Maria know that three weeks earlier, someone had donated a van for a single mom to receive.

"Maria, are you ready to ask for bread?"

Through her tears, she gave a muffled response, her heart crying out to God, "Yes, I am."

I reached into my desk drawer and pulled out the keys to the donated van. "Maria," I said, as I handed them to her across the desk, "these are keys given to you by God. I am just the delivery boy. This is how good your God is."

She looked up at me, makeup smearing her face, with shocked, hopeful eyes.

"Really? Is this really for me?" Then she hesitated for a moment. "But all of my stuff is in my friend's car."

"Let's go get it! It's a van. Everything will fit," I said, getting up and leading her outside. When she saw the van, she gasped and let out a cry. "It's white!"

I thought, *Oh, boy, I only have one color. This is a one day only sale.*

As she started weeping again, she whispered, "I always wanted a white car."

Maria learned a valuable lesson that day. God promises to meet our needs, not our greeds.

But not all my clients were single moms wanting BMW's. Some had much bigger problems.

"Racetrack Jack" always shuffled in every year for me to do his taxes. He was a curmudgeon; gruff, well-weathered, and short-tempered, with a voice that sounded like he was gargling rocks.

Jack lived at the race track. When he wasn't working at the horse track as a groom, he was there gambling or cashing other people's tickets for a 10 percent commission. He would wander in every year or so, plop down in the chair, and pull out a bag overflowing with tickets from the track. I explained to him that he had to pay taxes on all of this income, to which he would invariably reply, "Can't. Lost it all." We scrambled to file the necessary papers to keep Jack out of hot water and get him legal again.

One year he barged into the office unannounced, strands of his wild gray hair sticking straight up and swaying as he moved. He marched over to me and slapped a letter from the IRS down on my desk. I was incredibly busy with another client's business, and it bothered me that he was interrupting my work.

"Got a letter from the IRS!" he exclaimed, crossing his arms defiantly. As he stood there in front of me, I could tell that he didn't look the same as I had seen him before. His stomach appeared to be noticeably swollen, as he stooped over, holding on to his gut like it was causing him immense pain.

"Jack, what's the story? You okay?"

"I'm dyin'!"

"What do you mean, you're dying?"

"I'm dyin'. Got cancer. I'm gonna die," he said, matter-of-factly.

He could tell by the look on my face that I wasn't comprehending it.

"I got cancer. Went to the doctor. Told me I got the cancer," Jack said gruffly, motioning to his stomach and chest. "All over inside me. They can't even operate. Just gonna die. Six months they told me. And then I got this letter from the IRS."

"You got a letter from the IRS? Jack, listen to me. For ten years I have been doing your taxes and representing you. I've been your go-to guy for all this time and I've never steered you wrong. You need to listen to me right now. I'm going to give you advice that is going to be the most important thing you have ever heard. Sit down."

As he pressed himself into the chair, I took the letter he had given me and ripped it in two in front of him. When he saw that, he leaned out of the chair, trying to prevent me from ripping more and grabbing desperately at the pieces.

"You can't do that! What are you doing? You can't rip that up. Gimme …"

"Listen to me. The most important thing you can do right now is get right with your Maker."

"Whattya mean?" he yelled.

"You need to get right with the Creator of the universe. You are about to meet Him."

"I know I am," he croaked, his gravelly voice wavering a little. He settled back into the chair and stared at me intently, apparently shocked by my bluntness.

"Now, have I ever steered you wrong?"

"No, you haven't."

"Have I always done right by you?"

"Yes, you have."

"Have I waited for payment from you for months and forgiven debts from you?"

"Yes, sir, you have."

"So listen to me right now. Forget the IRS. I want you to focus on meeting your Maker. Let me tell you about Him. He forgives you, He loves you. He wants to have a relationship with you."

"Bah! He don't want me. He knows what I done."

"Yeah, He does know what you've done and He wants to forgive you right now. He wants you to ask for forgiveness. When you die, and you are going to die, you are going to meet Him and spend eternity there instead of hell. I want to see you there."

"Ah, skip the fire and brimstone, son."

"This isn't fire and brimstone, this is reality."

When he heard this he stopped talking, and for a moment, there was complete silence as he thought about what I was saying.

"What do I do?" he finally said, looking me squarely in the eyes with a scared and questioning face.

"If you want to accept His offer to you and invite Him to live inside you, just repeat after me as I pray with you."

I prayed with him for several minutes, as he accepted Jesus Christ as his Savior in front of me. As we prayed, Jack broke down, his massive shoulders heaving as he sobbed into his hands. When we had finished, he looked up at me, with tears streaming down his unshaven, scraggly face, and whispered, "I feel so much better, Kevin." The countenance on his face instantly changed to a look of incredible serenity, one that I will never forget.

"I want you to remember that there's nothing else you have to do. You've accepted Him as your Savior. Now I want you to get to know Him for these last few months. Will you do that?"

"Yes, I will. I am going to live with my daughter in Ohio," he said, writing down her address for me. "Can you help me get to know Him?"

"Of course, Jack. I will send you some books that will help you. I want you to have this as well," I said, handing him a Bible that was on my shelf.

We embraced and talked for several more minutes before he left. I watched him leave for the last time I would ever see him on this planet. As he meandered down the sidewalk, I could see a lightness in his step that wasn't there before. When I got back to my desk, I thanked God for interrupting my day. My work seemed so insignificant compared to the joy I was just privileged enough to partake in.

I picked up the piece of paper where Jack had written his daughter's address. Scribbled in small letters and barely legible, Jack's new address read: 120 Victory Lane.

---

Judy K. was a single mother who had moved to Florida with her kids. She had loaded all her stuff in her light blue Chrysler Concorde, with the hopes of getting into the real estate business. After several years of pounding the pavement, she became very successful, selling some of the top houses in South Florida.

Then, when the real estate bubble burst, she found herself working at a small local church at a much lower salary. However, she was still driving the sleek SUV that she had leased to show clients she was successful, which was costing her $1,000 per month for the car plus insurance.

When she came into my office for counseling, I told her she had to give up the car. Now, I was beginning to think that making single mothers cry was becoming a habit, because at this news, she immediately broke down and bawled.

"How big is your God?" I asked. "How big is your God?"

"My God is big," she sobbed. "But how am I going to get by now?"

"God is going to provide. Let's pray right now. 'Lord, we know you will never leave us or forsake us, and we know you will never leave or forsake Judy. We trust you to provide for us when we do the right thing. Please be with Judy in the coming months as she seeks to turn her life around, and let her do the right thing in your eyes, not the world's eyes.'"

Judy gave up the car and trusted God to provide for her. An acquaintance at work generously lent her a car to use for a couple weeks while she was looking for something in her price range.

Judy came into my office a few weeks later, wringing her hands in distress.

"I'm driving a borrowed car right now, and I am getting by," she sighed, "but I've already had it for three weeks, and I'm afraid I am taking advantage of my friend. I have been looking every day, but there is nothing I can afford. What can I do?"

"I've got an idea," I said, picking up the phone and calling the Sheridan House, a local ministry that sometimes provided cars for single moms.

"I have a single mother here who is doing the right thing. She is struggling right now, and faithfully took this car back that she couldn't afford. Do you guys have anything?"

"Right now we don't have anything. We just fixed up a car and gave it to a sweet lady last week, but right now we've got nothing. I'm so sorry."

"That's alright. I just thought I would check. Thanks anyway," I said, starting to hang up the phone.

I've learned that when circumstances don't seem to be working out, the evil one immediately puts a thought in your mind that God doesn't care about you, and that you're being naïve to believe that He will provide what you need.

The disappointment only lasted for about two seconds.

"Wait, Kevin!" I heard faintly coming from the receiver, stopping me hanging it up.

I pulled the phone back to my ear. "Yes?"

"My secretary is on the phone with somebody right now, who wants to give a car to a single mom. Can you believe it? The call came just when you were asking. Hang on a second. Can she come by tomorrow?"

When I gave Judy the good news, she cried for the second time in my office. At this point, I probably caused the highest concentration of single-mom-tears this side of the Mississippi. But this time, these were tears of joy.

A couple days later, Judy sent me a picture of her standing next to her new car. It was a light blue Chrysler Concorde, the same year, make, and model as the car she had before the SUV. What are the odds of that happening by chance?

After twenty years as their most famous Prodigal Son, I was invited back to my high school, Florida Bible, to speak to the students. I showed up on a rainy Friday night to see about 150 young people playing video games in the youth building, which was a warehouse painted much like the old punk clubs I used to frequent when I was a teen-ager. I sat in a back room, nervously listening to the piped-in sounds of the latest Christian rock bands.

They say the first two minutes are the most important for any speaker, and when kids are the audience, that number plummets to about thirty seconds. I wanted to capture their attention, but at the same time, had to avoid coming off as that guy who thinks he's relevant but is hopelessly lost. I didn't want them to view me as a washed-up parent, or lame preacher wagging my finger in disgust at youth I had never met.

As is my custom before speaking engagements, I prayed diligently that night, as the band brought the house down with covers of Sanctus Real, Switchfoot, and mewithoutYou. It's always hard to follow music, but as I prayed, I couldn't help but notice that this band had special talent.

I had to keep up with the tempo, so when I went out, I broke right into all the gory details of my arrest, the Mafia, the serial killer, and the ladies garden shoes. I told them about how I was betrayed, but how I was the biggest betrayer. I closed with an altar call, which is always a risky prospect for a preacher, and I challenged them to live a life that is set apart for God. I offered to give them "Live Original" armbands if they were serious about their commitment.

There was awkward silence until one courageous, young teenager came walking to the front, while the acoustic guitar quietly strummed. This guy seemed to break the ice, as other kids started following him, one by one, as young people from all nationalities and backgrounds came forward to get the "Live Original" armbands.

I prayed once again. This time it was a "You Rock, God" prayer to a great God, who used His hose to shower the truth on these youth. Whenever I speak, I always do it with the expectation that I am going to change the world. So, when I see people responding to what I'm saying, I turn into a wild man. This night was no different.

The following Sunday, I visited the church's worship service. A young kid, who looked to be about fifteen and sat a couple rows up from us, passed a note to me, as if we were back in school. I unfolded it and began reading. Seconds later, I was crying, putting my head down so no one would see my tears.

I slipped the note to Steph as gingerly as possible, concealing my treasured find. She read it with a stunned look on her face, and as she looked at me, I pointed toward the back of a kid who was sitting in the pew two rows up. I tried to explain the whole deal, but she was still reeling in bewilderment. This is what the letter said:

> You are such a great man. Because you are an influential person in my life. What I'm trying to say is that you never gave up on your life. I mean you accepted Christ in your life in your jail cell. And God helped you understand that he had a plan for your life, but the question is He really working in mine?
>
> Another thing I am trying to say is that God has put you in my life to help me understand life and how to wait patiently. I'm in a foster home and I think that God is giving up on me. So would you please pray for me? I cry every night to God so that I could just be in a family that loves me. Thanks for talking to me and thanks for being in my life.

Sincerely,
Dominic

Immediately following the service, I went to the foyer of the church hoping to catch a glimpse of Dominic. I wanted to tell him how much I was moved by his note, and that he was my hero because I admired his courageous heart. The kids who had heard me speak started mobbing me, wanting to meet me and shake my hand, but I kept looking around for Dominic.

Finally, I saw him out of the corner of my eye, waiting in the corner for his turn and looking down at his shoes. When he finally approached me, I grinned from ear to ear and blurted out how thankful I was to get his note. I tried to assure him that God was going to take care of him.

He politely listened, but it was clear that he was losing hope. I could see in his young, dejected face, the years of heartache he must have been through. His small body stood in stark contrast to his maturity, which was wise and hardened for his age.

After a moment or two, his house parent abruptly came and escorted him away in the middle of our conversation. As I briskly walked beside them, he called out, "Will you visit me?"

"Absolutely. I promise," I said, watching him disappear out of sight.

I found out he lived as a foster child in a community called "His House." It was a caring, loving place for orphans, which I had a natural aversion to, based on the horror stories my dad often recounted from his childhood.

I decided to bring him a T-shirt from my ministry, armbands, a book, M&M's, and some other stuff I thought a kid might think is cool. After arriving at the facility, I discovered that I couldn't get in because I hadn't been cleared. I was heartbroken because I was about to leave for London to tout my first book on the radio, and then to eastern Europe to visit some missionaries and family. This trip would keep me away for at least a month.

The thought of a devastated little Dominic sitting on his bunk waiting for me, thinking I would never come, just broke my heart into pieces. I called the social worker and explained the situation. She told me there was nothing I could do but to get clearance and then come back later. She promised to tell him I had stopped by and give him the goodies. I also gave her a handwritten note to deliver, in which I tried to explain that I would have jumped the electric fence if I knew I would have been able to see him.

As the next few months flew by, every time I thought of Dominic, I imagined his pain. Finally, I received the news that the clearance had come through. I'll have to admit I was a bit concerned that they might keep an ex-con out of an orphanage, and wondered how I would explain that to Dominic.

When I got there, it was as if Dominic and I were the best of friends and not a day had lapsed. He hugged me and laughed, and told me that my words had given him hope to keep trusting in God and not give up. He excitedly told me, with a giant smile on his face, that after a lifetime of waiting, he was finally getting adopted by a Christian family. He informed me about every detail of their lives and personalities, and what they were going to do together as a family.

I can't describe the relief this was to me, knowing that his future would be in good hands. I had told those kids on that Friday night that if they would place their complete trust in God, that He would provide for them. It takes faith to make that kind of promise, not knowing what's going on in their lives. In Dominic's case, God actually let me see that He had come through again.

One day I received a call from a couple named Bob and Michelle, who wanted to come in for counseling. I had met a friend of Bob and Michelle's at one of my events, and he told them about me. At first, their story seemed all too familiar— loss of income, mortgage troubles, and marital problems. Being a financial counselor sometimes throws you into the role of marriage counselor as well, but that's another story.

We agreed to meet at a little greasy spoon diner. I strolled in carrying a copy of my first book, which I give to everyone I counsel, and spotted a couple that had to be Bob and Michelle. I sat down, and we ordered a round of coffee as they ran down their story. I listened intently over the chatting at the other tables.

Bob spoke first. "You see, we were doing well. I own, uh, owned a rental property, a strip mall, over in the Naples area. I did what I thought everybody did. I refinanced every year. Well, you know, I thought it would keep going like it was," he said, staring down at his coffee and stirring it distractedly.

Opened in front of him was my book, *Building Your Financial Fortress in 52 Days*, like I had never seen it before—bent, dog-eared, highlighted, and notes written in the margins. I was extremely flattered, but I tried to remain cool, like I hadn't seen it.

"Everybody I knew was doing it," he said. "Anyway, my debt got too big to pay even the minimum payments. The bank used to let it slide from month to month. Problem is, they went out of business and the FDIC came in there. Needless to say, they didn't let *anything* slide. First time I couldn't pay, they stepped in and ordered all the tenants to pay everything directly to them. So, overnight, Michelle and I were left with nothing—no income, no real estate, no assets, no nothing."

"Everything's gone," Michelle echoed.

"Now, before you stop me," Bob continued, "I know now that this was all my doing. I should never have borrowed the way I did, but when you're in that lowly situation, it doesn't matter that much how you got there, you know what I mean? If anything, you're sadder because it was your own fault. When you've got somebody to blame, it's easier. I think. Maybe. Anyway, I was desperate. So desperate. It seemed like there was no hope of ever getting out of it."

Michelle interjected, "One day he just left. He bought a gun, took $2,000 from our account, and walked out."

"I just left. I thought things would be better for her. I checked into a motel on the water, and was trying to get up the courage to, you know, do it," Bob said matter-of-factly.

I could see tears welling up in Michelle's eyes as Bob relived this. The wounds were still fresh. They stung. She dabbed at her eyes with a small handkerchief she had pulled from her purse.

"I just hunkered down and tried to do it. I almost pulled the trigger many times, but something stopped me," he said, staring off in the distance, his mind obviously in that motel room.

Michelle jumped in. "I was desperate and at my wits end. I decided to go to the bookstore to look through their financial books, and that's when I found yours," she said. "I bought it and went down to the motel where I knew he was. He didn't want to talk, but I just left the book there and prayed."

Bob rubbed her arm lovingly and continued, "Man, I picked up the book on a whim. I didn't want to, you know? I read the first chapter, and it was my style. It was short," he smiled. "You were talking in there about how you were arrested and up to your eyeballs in debt with no hope, and I saw myself in there. I wrote on the bottom, 'This is me! This is my life.'"

He grabbed the book and turned to the last page of the first chapter to show me. There were so many notes I had to look for it.

"I know it's supposed to be just one chapter a day, like a journey or something, but I just kept reading. I couldn't stop. I felt like I was you, and I saw how God gave you hope, so I knew there was hope for me. Man, I cried like a baby. I prayed to God like you did, and told Him I trusted Him. I rededicated myself to Him. I threw away the gun and called Michelle to apologize."

"He called me to apologize," Michelle echoed, with a sigh of relief. "I was just so elated to have him back."

I sat in stunned silence for several seconds, not knowing what to say. *This is what life is all about. This is the Life that is truly Life*, I thought. I helped them get on a financial plan that would get their debt under control, and prayed with them that they would stick to it.

As I left the diner, it dawned on me that I was still repaying what I had stolen, except in a different way. I had caused financial problems by embezzling hundreds of thousands of dollars, and now God had "sentenced" me to life—a life of helping others get out of their financial problems.

This life of counseling others was more exciting than when I was embezzling from the Sheriff. I never knew where my next "assignment from God" would come from. Sometimes He would arrange an appointment in ways that I could not have planned.

One time I decided to buy a second car for our family that one of my employees was selling. It was a Honda Civic with 130,000 miles and the only thing wrong with it was that the plastic "H" on the front of the car was missing. Now, most women would probably have no problem with this fact, but as a man, I was feeling a little emasculated and vulnerable driving around without a plastic "H" on the hood of my car.

I went to the dealership and bought a plastic "H" for $20. I tried every way possible to put it on the car, but no matter which way I turned it, it wouldn't fit. When I took it back to the dealership, they informed me I had an after-market grill and that's why it didn't work. Although they gave me the $20 back, I was still bummed.

"Thanks a lot, God," I prayed. "I just wanted to do something small for myself, and I can't even do that. I'm even getting ready to do a Crown Financial Seminar to help your people. I mean, c'mon God. What difference is $20 going to make?"

When I got back to the office, I gave my secretary the $20, begrudgingly instructing her to use it as a free scholarship for someone to come to my Crown Financial Ministries event the next week in Tampa.

During the lunch break of the event, a woman in her thirties approached me. I could see from her face that she had been crying. I thought she might be a single mom, based on my past experiences with them.

"Kevin," she said between sniffles, "I was the recipient of the scholarship today."

"Well, that's great. I'm so glad," I said, nonchalantly. "We weren't sure if anybody was ..."

She interrupted me, "And I gave my heart to Jesus today."

"Don't stand too close. I'm going to get hit by lightning," I said, realizing my own shortsightedness. I wanted to use my $20 for a piece of plastic, and God wanted to send someone to Heaven with it!

What if God wants us to do something more meaningful with our cash, our cars, our houses, our retirement accounts, our resources, or our time, for something more satisfying than what our agenda tells us? What pleasure we may be missing out on because we opted for the big screen TV, or leather seats, or a little piece of plastic for the front of our car. The joy I would have received from that plastic "H" can't even begin to compare to how I felt with a crying woman in front of me, telling me she was going to spend eternity with me in Heaven because of $20.

Jesus said in Luke 16:9, "I tell you, use worldly wealth to gain friends for yourself, so that when it is gone, you will be welcomed into eternal dwellings." When I get to Heaven, God isn't going to say, "Dude, that was a sweet 'H' on your car." He's going to say, "This is Donna. She is here because of you. Well done."

Donna continued, "I've been struggling a lot lately. I'm the only one working. My husband was arrested and now he can't find a job. He is so discouraged. His name is Kevin."

*What a coincidence*, I thought. "Was your husband by any chance, me?"

She giggled a little, wiping a stray tear from her cheek. "No, but we liked the name so much that we named our son Kevin as well. We have a daughter as well. Her name is Kevina."

I thought God must have been putting me on. This must be His version of *Candid Camera*. He was up there with the angels, munching popcorn, and laughing hysterically at the scene He had set, millennia ago, to unfold for me.

"I called the church from a pay phone when I saw the sign for your event. I didn't have the $20 to get in, but I thought maybe there was an off chance they would do a discounted rate or something. I didn't have much hope, but I called and they said they had just gotten a scholarship for someone to come for free. This has been so good for me to hear that we can have a life without the pain from money that we are experiencing."

We talked for several minutes and I told her that I would be willing to talk to her and her husband sometime.

A few days later, I sent her an email:

> Tell Kevin I feel his pain, have walked in his shoes, and I have experienced righteous anger on his behalf for the way he is being treated. God will never treat him this way. I had to start my own business because I was in the same boat as your husband. God has done great things with my life since then. Kevin, maybe God is leading you to the next level to a small business out of your car or your bedroom. That is where I started, scared and hungry. Just remember, the object of your faith, Jesus Christ, is rich and generous.

She replied the same day:

> Dear Kevin,
> I believe you shared this with me despite your flesh telling you not to. Thank you for blessing me and my husband. I thank God for the day you bought a plastic "H" that didn't fit, and that got me a scholarship to attend your event. I intend to share this email with my husband, praying that it will give him the encouragement that has escaped him for so long. Maybe, if you would allow it, I could have you and my Kevin speak on the telephone.

He is weak right now and I am sure I don't help at all complaining about the bills, but through speaking to you, I am praying for a breakthrough in my life where I will stop focusing on my circumstances and start focusing on God's love.

Donna

To this day, whenever I drive that Honda Civic, I think about the people that will be in heaven because I couldn't make the plastic "H" fit.

It's fun to watch God provide for people in ways we don't expect. I found my next appointment through a radio broadcast that I was doing.

Every tax season, I'm asked to come on several radio shows and talk about taxes, usually on April 14 and 15. I warn everyone to get their taxes done and sent off before "The Service" comes and gets them. One year, I was on "KISS Country" in South Florida when a man named Joe Taylor heard me on the radio. He came in the next day to get his taxes done. As we were looking over his wife's W2, I noticed something familiar.

"CSCA? What does that stand for?" I asked, trying to place it.

"That's the Coral Springs Christian Academy," he replied. "My wife is a teacher out there."

"Yeah. Coral Springs Christian Academy," I said slowly, looking up as if the ceiling held the answers. "Was that the school, um, was there a teacher out there who might have been dying of cancer or something?"

"Yeah, that was my wife's best friend," Joe said morosely.

"Really? Whatever happened to her?"

"Well, she died."

"Oh, wow. I'm sorry. That's awful."

"Yeah, that woman and that family, they really brought us to a point where we could … well, you see, I haven't really been talking much with my daughter. I have two daughters, Stacy and Annabelle. Stacy plays soccer and I love that. We have a lot to talk about. A lot in common. But Annabelle, well, she's really involved in the youth group at church and I don't do that much with her. She likes to get involved in charity and stuff like that, and I don't really believe in those things.

"Stacy just went off to college, so now it is just Annabelle at home, and we just sort of avoid each other. Anyway, Cathy was my wife's best friend. My wife and some of the teachers at the school wanted to do something for her, something monetary, because they had a lot of medical bills and she was leaving the job, and her husband was out of work ..."

"Her husband was out of work? What were their names?"

"Mike and Cathy ...," he started.

"Moriarty?"

"Yeah, yeah. Mike and Cathy Moriarty."

Now I knew why the story sounded familiar. I went to a treasure chest in my office that held all the letters I received from people I had counseled. I opened it up and fished through it until I found what I was looking for.

"A few months ago, maybe about six months now, a man came in and he was looking for a job," I began. "He was doing a bunch of odd jobs, not making a whole heckuva lot of money, and he was way behind on his bills. He came in for some financial counseling. He said to me, 'Kevin, I heard that you do counseling. That's why I'm here. I'm working about thirty hours a week right now, but I have a chance to get a second job for another thirty or forty so I can pay some medical bills for my wife. You see, she's been diagnosed with cancer and they've given her six months to live.'

"I thought for a minute and then prayed with him. I prayed for wisdom because in James 1 it says you just have to ask for wisdom, and here you go. It's kind of cool. Anyway, I'm praying for wisdom, but the whole time I'm doubting a little. I don't know what to tell this guy, you know? I mean, what would you say?"

"Man," Joe said, shaking his head, "you got me on that one."

"When I finished praying, though, it came to me. I said to him, 'You love your wife. I can tell. You are practically in tears in front of me.' And he said, 'Yeah, I love her dearly. We've been married for twenty-five years.' I said to him, 'You know what, Michael? You need to spend every moment you have with Cathy. Every waking moment. Right now, there is a great sense of urgency to spend every moment with that gift that may not be here in a year. If there is a bill that doesn't get paid, it doesn't get paid.' He said, 'Yeah, but what if they take my car?'"

"It wasn't easy, but I told him, 'They could take your car. They may take away your credit. They may hound you. One day there will be a time to pay all those things. Right now, focus on your wife. But listen to me closely: do not go into debt, do not borrow. When you need something, get on your knees and start praying. Absolutely do not borrow. You are going to do both things I am telling you. You are not going to work more hours, and you are not going to borrow.'"

Joe leaned forward in his chair, riveted by what I was saying.

"He protested," I explained. "He fought me, saying, 'But I need money right now. How am I going to survive?' I asked him what I ask everybody, 'How big is your God?' and he said, 'My God is big.' He started to cry. And he is one big guy, you know."

"Yes, he is," Joe agreed.

"I read him this passage from Matthew 6:28-33," I said, grabbing my Bible.

*See how the lilies grow. They do not labor or spin. Yet I tell you, not even Solomon in all his splendor was dressed like one of these. If that is how God clothes the grass of the field, which is here today, and tomorrow is thrown into the fire, how much more will he clothe you, O you of little faith! And do not set your heart on what you will eat or drink; do not worry about it. For the pagan world runs after all such things, and your Father knows that you need them. But seek his kingdom, and these things will be given to you as well.*

"He left and we sent him some Publix gift cards about a week later. I think it's because I was trying to rescue God. Maybe I didn't fully believe what I was telling him, so I thought I'd send him something in case God didn't come through, right? Well, a few weeks later, I got this letter."

I held it up for him and began reading.

> Dear Kevin,
>
> First and foremost, I want to thank you for your inspiration. You are truly doing Christ's work. The generous gift of Publix gift cards was another blessing. My words cannot really express my thanks for them. But your greatest gift to me is your example of faith. You knew that God would hear my prayers and provide what is needed. I suspect that you called someone at Coral Springs Christian Academy. Why would you not? It is another way you could help us. The community at Coral Springs Christian Academy has gotten together and brought us wonderful meals and innumerable Christmas gifts for a beloved teacher. They also handed my wife Cathy an envelope with over $4,000 in it. You are opening my eyes wide.
>
> Like Jesus said, "Oh you of little faith! And do not set your heart on what you will eat or drink; do not worry about it. For the pagan world runs after all such things, and your Father knows that you need them. But seek his kingdom, and these things will be given to you as well."
>
> Merry Christmas and a happy and blessed New Year.
> Michael and Cathy Moriarty

I put the letter back on the table and looked up to see Joe on the verge of tears.

"Joe, here's the thing. *I never called Coral Springs Christian Academy*. That was God."

"Wow," he sighed, blinking to keep the tears from coming. "I remember my wife and Annabelle making meals and getting Christmas gifts for them and I remember my wife giving most of her salary to them. She usually doesn't tell me how much she gives because I just don't do those things. I don't believe in it."

Then, almost in an inaudible way, he whispered, "I do now."

God was letting me in on the back end of a miracle, and I felt like I was seeing something I wasn't supposed to see. A veil where God was working had opened a crack and I peered in to see something so infinite that mortal eyes are not meant to witness it.

We sat in silence for a moment, and then Joe spoke up.

"I think I know how to connect with Annabelle now. She loves giving. She loves mission trips. She loves making cakes to raise money for people going to Haiti. She loves to do stuff like that," he said, his face lighting up. "I'm going to help her make those cakes. I'm going to go volunteer with her at the charity she always goes to. I'm going to give to her youth group's projects. Maybe I'll even send her on a mission trip. She would love that!"

Joe left the office like a new man, animated and with eyes shining at the prospect of a new start for himself and his daughter.

And I sat back and marveled at what God had done, in spite of my attempts to rescue Him.

Berni was a single mother whose husband had left her with three small children to raise. She first came to me for counseling in 1993, and I saw her again a number of times for about ten years. Every time she came in, she would show me a new credit card bill that she had incurred for food, school, clothes, or car repairs. Every time I would tell her to pay them off and get rid of them, but it was hard for me to blame her. She wasn't buying extravagant things; these were groceries, rent on her hovel of an apartment in the seedy area of town, and a pizza every once in a while.

My family and I used to send Christmas gifts to their family every year. We often tried to be an encouragement to Berni, whose load was so heavy. We became close to their kids, and as they grew up I attended their weddings. They later came and thanked me for encouraging their mother through the hard times.

In 2004, Berni got married, and she and her new husband asked me to counsel them on joining their finances. I told them they had to rearrange their lifestyles so that they could live on just one salary, and then save the other's income in the bank.

At first they protested, but finally followed my advice to downsize, get out of debt, and start saving. They came back a year later asking for advice about a large check Berni's husband had received for his first real estate sale. They told me that their church, Miami Vineyard, was taking up a big offering in a couple weeks and they wanted to help, but were scared. I told them to just give it to the offering and trust God to use it properly.

Around the same time, another couple from Miami Vineyard came in for counseling. I helped them get out of the trouble they were in, and convinced them to turn back to giving. I thought it was strange that two couples from the same small church thirty miles away had come in to see me. *What are you working on, God?* I wondered.

Later that year, Berni sent me a CD with a little note attached to it: "Kevin, I was led to share this CD with you. I don't know why, but God does. I pray it will be a blessing."

I threw it into my pile of never-listened-to sermon CDs, and didn't think about it again until she started calling me every day to ask if I had heard it. To appease her, I popped it in the CD player and listened. The quality was awful. I heard the pastor from Miami Vineyard talking about playing a video from an offering they had done the week before.

The pastor, Kevin Fisher, had challenged the congregation to collect an offering—not for their own church, but to give away to a small inner-city church called Centro Christiano Casablanca. For several weeks, the members of the church scrimped, saved, and sacrificed to make the offering a memorable one.

The day finally came to deliver the sacrificial offering to the other church. Three hundred adrenalin-filled members of Miami Vineyard formed a caravan of cars, vans, and buses, and drove to the inner city church. Inside the small building, a group of eight unsuspecting people were praying, huddled around a board with three words scribbled on it: "God will provide."

Suddenly, the church doors burst open and a multitude of people from the Vineyard hurried in and filled up seats. Their bodies packed the modest church, as their applause, whistling, and laughing reached a deafening pitch.

As if on cue, a hush came over the audience as the stunned pastor of the inner city church, Eddie Rivera, made his way to the stage. He grabbed a microphone and said to the Pastor of Miami Vineyard, "Pastor, I just want to know what is going on!" He had no idea they had been "invaded" by another church.

Pastor Kevin from the Vineyard took the microphone from Pastor Eddie's hand and jokingly announced to the anxious crowd, "In the words of the great theologians, The Blues Brothers, 'We're on a mission from God!'"

The nervous excitement could no longer be held back, and the house of worship erupted in an awe-inspiring uproar of screams, cheers, and shouts.

Pastor Kevin reached into his pocket and pulled out the envelope that contained the offering his congregation had collected for the inner-city church. Pastor Eddie's next words were barely audible, as he opened the envelope and read: "It is more blessed to give than receive. Here is your check for $57,000." These last words came out fitfully as he fought back the tears.

Tears of exuberant joy began to flow down the faces of too many to count. No one at Miami Vineyard knew this, but this little church was on the verge of closing its doors and Pastor

Eddie had not been paid for six months. The generous offering from one church to another had come just in the nick of time.

An air conditioning repairman, who was not a Christian, happened to be at the church that morning, fixing their broken air conditioning unit. He was so moved by this selfless act, he gave his life to the Lord that very day.

When I heard that this entire event was recorded on a video, I went on an unstoppable mission to get my hands on it. I called Miami Vineyard and asked if they could send me a copy of the video of the offering giveaway.

The guy on the other line, Nick Korba, said, "Well, we really don't have extra copies of it. It's more just for internal purposes."

I said, completely serious, "I'll give you guys a thousand dollars for that video."

Nick paused on the other end. "You want us to overnight it to you? I'll drive it up to you myself. What format do you want it in?"

It was the best thousand dollars I have ever spent. I have shown that video to hundreds of thousands of people through my events and my website, www.account417.com. Everyone who sees it is moved beyond words, and thousands have given their lives to Christ after witnessing this incredible act of love. It has had an exponential effect. Many churches have watched the video and decided to do an offering giveaway themselves.

The Vineyard and many other churches are following after the Apostle Paul when he urged the Macedonians to collect money for another congregation. They are living like the early church:

> *All the believers were one in heart and mind. No one claimed that any of his possessions was his own, but they shared everything they had. With great power the apostles continued to testify to the resurrection of the Lord Jesus, and much grace was upon them all. There were no needy persons among them. For from time to time those who owned lands or houses sold them, brought the money*

*from the sales and put it at the apostles' feet, and it was distributed to anyone as he had need.* (Acts 4:32-35)

After this, Bernie got it. She witnessed firsthand the joyful life of giving that God wants for everyone as we follow His awesome plan. It was a wakeup call for me too.

The incredible life-change I witnessed through my speaking events and counseling filled me with a joy and a purpose that I had never felt before. I knew God was calling me for something greater when He took away the joy of just working my business. I was starting to pay more attention to the tax code than His code, and it was time for a change.

I read Randy Alcorn's *The Treasure Principle*, which completely transformed my life. I decided to sell the house and my tax business I had worked so hard for, which had grown to seven employees. Then I moved my little family, Stephanie, Rachel, and Ethan, into a small apartment to free up all of our resources to start a ministry. I founded "Account417," which is based on Philippians 4:17, NASB: "Not that I seek the gift itself, but I seek for the profit which increases to your account."

My one and only goal is to help others avoid the pitfalls of greed, debt, and discontentedness. I had fallen into all three traps. Greed motivated me to steal all the money I could so I could fulfill my foolish cravings. When that didn't satisfy, I got into debt so I could take hold of the American Dream. And discontentment created an appetite that couldn't be satisfied. I found myself wrapped up with a heavy, burdensome life, toiling my life away just to get a big house, a fast car, and a phony reputation.

I learned from experience that chasing after these things never made me happy. If they had, I would still be doing them. Instead, I discovered that following God offered so much more, and it will go on forever.

# CHAPTER 13

# living on the edge of the miraculous

As you can tell from reading my story, I'm not the same person now that I was at the beginning of this book. God has taken me from being someone who was enslaved to greed, to a person who knows the joy of being radically generous. How did that happen? I finally came to the place where I turned my life completely over to God.

God is generous by nature and it only makes sense that when He operates in our lives, we, too, will freely help others. He calls each of us to follow in His footsteps and not trust in money. First Timothy 6:17-19 says:

> Command those who are rich in this present world not to be arrogant nor to put their hope in wealth, which is so uncertain, but to put their hope in God, who richly provides us with everything for our enjoyment. Command them to do good, to be rich in good deeds, and to be generous and willing to share. In this way they will lay up treasure for themselves as a firm foundation for the coming age, so that they may take hold of the life that is truly life.

You probably don't consider yourself wealthy. When you think of the word "rich," people like Oprah or Warren Buffett pop into your mind. But you, in fact, are richer than most people who have ever lived on Earth. Consider the following facts. Only 7 percent of the people currently on this planet have a car. Do you have a car?

The dollar amount needed to provide basic education, sanitation, health, and nutrition for every developing impoverished country in the world, about $28 billion, is the amount Americans spend each year on ice cream. We spend $600 billion on cars, $250 billion on Christmas gifts, $110 billion on fast food, and another $33 billion on weight loss products, contrasted with an embarrassing $39 million on missions. Half the world, that's more than three billion people, live on less than $2.50 a day. It's easy to feel poor when you see your neighbor or some celebrity having even more, but you have to remember that *your* little world is not *the* world.

So, if we accept the premise that Americans and Europeans are the very tip of the financial pyramid in this world, and if we take God's Word seriously, it follows that we must also be generous. And I'm not talking about the tithe.

In my "Margin and Meaning" event, I never, ever use the word "tithe." I find it so narrow in scope that it hinders the attitude of openness God is calling us to live with. He doesn't want us to treat His money as another line in the budget, a halfhearted obligation. This is about taking Jesus' words seriously and bringing food to the poor, clothing the naked, taking up the causes of the oppressed and needy, getting involved in social causes in His name.

It's not always a comfortable life, but it's a joyous one. As John Piper has said, "A $100,000 salary must not be accompanied by a $100,000 lifestyle. God has made us to be conduits of his grace, not cul-de-sacs. The danger is in thinking the conduit should be lined with gold. It shouldn't. Copper will do. No matter how grateful we are, gold will not make the world think our God is good; it will make people think that our god is gold."[1]

We must not be arrogant or put our hope in wealth, rather we should put our trust in God, who promises to always provide for our needs. We are also called to be "generous and willing to share" in order to lay up treasure for ourselves in a place where there is never a recession or a depression. If God's promise to us were only eternal rewards, it would be an incredible offer in itself, but He tells us we can also take hold of "the life that is truly life" while we are here on Earth.

This way of life is actually the only way you'll be fulfilled. Also in 1 Timothy 6:6-10, God tells us:

*But godliness with contentment is great gain. For we brought nothing into the world, and we can take nothing out of it. But if we have food and clothing, we will be content with that. People who want to get rich fall into temptation and a trap and into many foolish and harmful desires that plunge men into ruin and destruction. For the love of money is a root of all kinds of evil. Some people, eager for money, have wandered from the faith and pierced themselves with many griefs.*

God offers us a contented life, a life free from the financial pain and heartache that the world offers. Soren Kierkegaard, the famed Danish theologian and philosopher, said, "Riches and abundance come hypocritically clad in sheep's clothing pretending to be security against anxieties and they then become the object of anxiety.... They secure a man against anxieties about as well as the wolf which is put to tending the sheep secures them ... against the wolf."[2]

Maybe you're saying to yourself, "Well, how generous do I have to be? I already give my tithe and to a couple charities. You don't expect me to go without, do you?" My answer to this is *absolutely*. C.S. Lewis put it eloquently:

Some people nowadays say that charity ought to be unnecessary and that instead of giving to the poor we ought to be producing a society in which there were no poor to give to. They may be quite right in saying that we ought to produce this kind of society. But if anyone thinks that, as a consequence, you can stop giving in the meantime, then he has parted company with all Christian morality. I do not believe one can settle how much we ought to give. I am afraid the only safe rule is to give more than we can spare. In other words, if our expenditure on comforts, luxuries, amusements, etc., is up to the standard common among those with the same income as our own, we are probably giving away too little. If our charities do not at all pinch or hamper us, I should say they are too small. There ought to be things we should like to do and cannot do because our charities expenditure excludes them.[3]

This is not a "give until it hurts," lock all the doors and pass the plate because the pastor needs some alligator shoes type of plea. This is more like "give until it feels good." God already owns everything, so He doesn't need anything we have, but He wants to fill us with all joy and peace as we trust in Him.

He knows that a lifestyle of getting bigger and better cars, houses, trinkets, and wasting our lives accumulating everything the world tells us we need is never going to satisfy. He's saying that this lifestyle of radiant, joyful generosity is going to make you happier than anything you'll find in Wal-Mart, Home Depot, or the Mercedes dealership.

When you get to Heaven, do you think God is going to say, "Wow, that amazing fountain you had in your front yard led so many people to me. Let me introduce you to them! And your BMW M5 was such a witness to your neighbors that they all gave their hearts to me at the sight of it."

It's probably going to go something more like this: "You missed the whole point of what it means to know me. You've wasted your life."

I'm reminded of the final scene of *Schindler's List*, where Oscar Schindler is surrounded by the myriad of Jews he saved. His final thoughts were not of rejoicing as he looked at his nice watch and fancy car. But rather, he thought, *Why did I keep the car? That's ten people right there. People who are dead.*

Our charge is even graver than Schindler's. The way we use God's money cannot only mean the difference between life and death on this Earth, but also it can and does mean the difference between an eternity in hell or Heaven. Jesus said in Luke 16:9: "Use worldly wealth [money] to gain friends for yourselves so when it is gone you will be welcomed into eternal dwellings." Imagine getting to your eternal home in Heaven and being welcomed by the many people who made it in because of the money you gave. How does that compare to having a nice car or house for ten years?

Missionary Chet Bitterman couldn't wait to go on his first linguistic mission with Wycliffe Bible Translators. He prayed, "Lord, the tribe that's the most remote, the most difficult to reach because of location and culture, the tribe no one else might select because of those reasons, Lord, if it's okay with you, that's my tribe."

Wycliffe sent him to the most remote tribe in Columbia, the Carijona. On January 19, 1981, at 6:30 in the morning, the doorbell rang at the Bittermans' house. Seven terrorists, all armed, burst through the door, demanding to see the SIL director. When informed that he wasn't there, the rebels pointed at Chet, "We'll take you." Before being marched out the rear office at gunpoint, Chet kissed and held his two daughters, Esther and Anna.

The terrorists made their demands known four days later: Wycliffe must abandon all activity and leave the country. Aside from a couple letters, a picture in the paper, and an audiotape, Chet's whereabouts were unknown for forty-eight days. On March 7, police found Chet's body in a parked bus south of Bogota. There were no signs of torture, just one shot to the chest. He was buried in Loma Linda.

Chet's martyrdom was not in vain. Instead of scaring applicants away from Wycliffe, the persecution actually sparked an increase in interest. In the year following Chet's sacrificial death, applications for Wycliffe's overseas ministries doubled. Two years after the kidnapping, one of the rebels told a Colombian pastor that he had given his life to Jesus Christ because of Chet Bitterman.

Jesus said, "Truly, truly, I say to you, unless a grain of wheat falls into the earth and dies, it remains alone; but if it dies, it bears much fruit" (John 12:24, NASB). God's request for generosity seems so small in light of these myriad of great people that came before us and so willing gave up their lives for the cause of Christianity. Hebrews 12:1 says, "Therefore, since we are surrounded by such a great cloud of witnesses, let us throw off everything that hinders and the sin that so easily entangles, and let us run with perseverance the race marked out for us."

This global mission of changing lives could actually be accomplished by making a decision to shun debt. We could divert the funds we are now sending to credit card companies and banks, to the tune of 1.3 trillion dollars ($2.6 trillion consumer debt divided by 51.3 percent Protestant Christians), to spreading the gospel. Even if we kept our lifestyles exactly the same, getting rid of debt and using God's money for His purposes instead of our own would result in such a monumental paradigm shift. The world would have to stand up and take notice of what God's people were doing.

You may think, as I did, that if we can trust God to provide for us, then why can't we trust Him to pay off our credit card bills? George Muller, a man responsible for hundreds of thousands of conversions, also cared for 10,024 orphans during his lifetime. When he started in 1838, there were accommodations for only 3,600 orphans in all of England. By the end of his life, he built orphanages to take care of these abandoned children, and he *never used credit*. God always supplied exactly what he needed. When he was asked about it, this was his reply:

But perhaps it may be asked, "Why do you not take the bread on credit? What does it matter whether you pay immediately for it, or at the end of the month, or the quarter, or the half year?" Seeing that the Orphan Houses are the work of the Lord, may you not trust in him that he will supply you with means to pay the bills which you contract with the butcher, baker, grocer, etc., as the things which you purchase are needful? My reply is this:

1. If the work in which we are engaged is indeed the work of God, then he whose work it is, is surely able and willing to provide the means for it.

2. But not only so, he will also provide the means at the time when they are needed. I do not mean that he will provide them when we think that they are needed; but yet that when there is real need, such as the necessaries of life being required, he will give them; and on the same ground on which we suppose we do trust in God to help us to pay the debt which we now contract, we may and ought to trust in the Lord to supply us with what we require at present, so that there may be no need for going into debt.

3. It is true, I might have goods on credit, and to a very considerable amount; but, then, the result would be, that the next time we were again in straits, the mind would involuntarily be turned to further credit which I might have, instead of being turned to the Lord, and thus faith, which is kept up and strengthened only by being *exercised*, would become weaker and weaker, till at last, according to all human probability, I should find myself deeply in debt and have no prospect of getting out of it.

4. Faith has to do with the word of God, rests upon the written word of God; but there is no promise that he will pay our debts. The word says rather, "Owe no man anything;" whilst there is the promise given to his children, "I will never leave thee nor forsake thee."[4]

The way we handle money is incredibly important to God. In fact, His Word talks about money and possessions in about 2,350 verses, more than any other subject except the Kingdom of God. If you have a red letter edition Bible and you didn't want to hear Jesus' words on the subject, you would have to rip out one-third of those red words.

These verses, though, are not there to harm us or make us live a monotonous, bland life. What we have is an incredible contract from God. It's what He wants *for us*, and not what He wants *from us*:

He is offering us the job of manager of what He provides us with. We just have to follow His accounting rules: no debt or love of money.

He will provide everything we *need* and even things we don't.

He will take away the pain of doing money the world's way and give us a life of pleasure, satisfaction, contentedness, and joy.

John Piper refers to this as "Christian Hedonism," a way of life that not only praises God, but brings us pure, selfish pleasure as well. Again, C.S. Lewis states:

> If there lurks in most modern minds the notion that to desire our own good and to earnestly hope for the enjoyment of it is a bad thing, I suggest that this notion has crept in from Kant and the Stoics and is no part of the Christian faith. Indeed, if we consider the unblushing promises of reward and the staggering nature of the rewards promised in the Gospels, it would seem that our Lord finds our desires, not too strong, but too weak. We are half-hearted creatures, fooling around with drink and sex and ambition when infinite joy is offered us, like an ignorant child who wants to go on making mud pies in a slum because he cannot imagine what is meant by the offer of a holiday at the sea. We are far too easily pleased.[5]

If my story has lent any weight to my words, I use it now for this simple plea: don't settle for a colorless, dead, mind-numbing life of mortgages, televisions, fabrics, electrical can openers, cars, fountains, low interest loans, striped wallpapers, manicured lawns, computers, leather interiors, sectional sofas, golfing trips, watches, 401Ks, pedicures, boats, strip malls, paint jobs, matching luggage sets, or any other depressing inanity that may apply.

Embrace a new way of living that is light, and free from heavy burdens: an original life lived like you are spending eternity someplace other than here. A life filled with light and love, bread and mercy, life change, heart change, grace, simplicity, generosity, charity, blessings, tears, joy, communion, elation, and most of all, pleasure.

That's what I wish for you, my friend.

### ENDNOTES

1   Piper, John. *Desiring God.* Sisters, Oregon: Multnomah Publishers, 1986, 173

2   Foster, Richard. *The Freedom of Simplicity*, New York, NY: HarperCollins, 1981, 88.

3   *Mere Christianity*, 86.

4   Muller, George. *The Life of Trust.* Boston, MA: Gould and Lincoln, 1861, 242.

5   C. S. Lewis Sermon, Oxford, England 1942.

# epilogue

Over two decades have passed since the embezzlement took place. My story wouldn't be complete without telling you what has happened to the other people mentioned in this book.

Paul married his girlfriend and has not talked with me since 1988. Rumor has it that his jet black hair is long gone and he now has a shaved head.

Tommy and Jason Tomaleri both graduated from law school and became criminal defense lawyers representing the worst kind of offenders and lawbreakers.

Donny Rocket never married, struggles with excess drinking, and has not spoken to me since the trial.

Monica found a new love, fled to Canada, and only called once since the ordeal.

Phyllis Carbo, who reminded me of Greta Garbo, didn't show up for work one day at the Sheriff's Office. She had died and in her will left most of her possessions to her dogs, Fupsy and Conner.

Gilmar and Jurema Gomes were forced to close down the Bancor business and have retired to Brazil.

Dave, the missionary pilot, got married to a woman who had gone to the jungles as a missionary. After they were married,

Stephanie and I visited them in Ecuador and we became close friends. Dave was killed one evening when his plane crashed during a terrible storm as he was trying to rescue someone.

My wonderful wife, Stephanie, helps me raise our children Rachel and Ethan, and is an incredible support to me in my endeavor to share Christ with the world.

Sheriff Nick Navarro failed to get re-elected and started a security firm specializing in protection services. In 2008, twenty years after my arrest, I arranged a meeting with the most powerful sheriff in this generation so I could apologize to him face-to-face. He accepted my request for forgiveness and complimented me for changing my ways and helping others. The video of this encounter can be seen at www.embezzlementbook.com.

To this day, I still don't know who tipped off the cops. To the person I would just like to say, "Thank you."

# bibliography

C. S. Lewis Sermon, Oxford, England 1942.

Foster, Richard. *The Freedom of Simplicity,* New York, NY: HarperCollins, 1981.

Lewis, C. S. *Mere Christianity.* New York, NY: HarperCollins, 1952.

Muller, George. *The Life of Trust.* Boston, MA: Gould and Lincoln, 1861.

Piper, John. *Desiring God.* Sisters, Oregon: Multnomah Publishers, 1986.

# Experience Victory Over Financial Problems

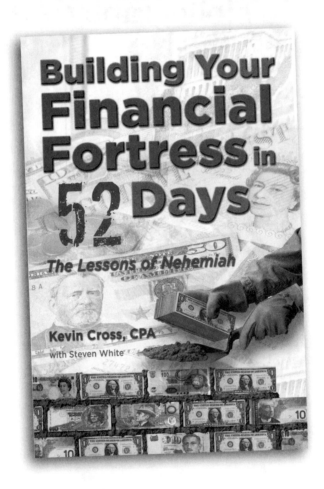

Learn the same principles Kevin used to get out of debt with this original and practical approach to biblical money management. He'll show you how to live in true financial freedom and peace.

ISBN# 978-0-88270-643-6 / 6 x 9 / 184 pages / $14.99

## Available in fine bookstores or at
### www.account417.com